A New Dawn
For America:
The Libertarian Challenge

A New Dawn For America:

The Libertarian Challenge

by

Roger L. MacBride

Green Hill Publishers, Inc.
Ottawa, Ill. 61350

A NEW DAWN FOR AMERICA: The Libertarian Challenge

© 1976 Roger L. MacBride

Green Hill Publishers, Inc.
Post Office Box 738
Ottawa, Illinois 61350

Manufactured in the United States of America.

ISBN: 0-916054-06-3

Special Dedication

I have a very special, personal debt to Rose Wilder Lane, the author of *The Discovery of Freedom*. Rose was my grandmother. I adopted her and she adopted me.

I met her when I was sixteen. My father, an editor of the *Reader's Digest*, was at the time condensing Rose's great novel about hard times, *Let the Hurricane Roar* (my partner and I have now created the television production YOUNG PIONEERS based upon it). One Sunday he took our family to have lunch with her at the White Turkey Inn in Danbury, Connecticut. Fabulous occasion. I was fascinated by her mind, and jumped at her offer to correspond. I wrote her, asking, I'm sure, the most naive questions. She patiently replied in ways that gave me new insights. Over a period, Rose unfolded for me the meaning of personal liberty, and of freedom as part of our nature. She drew on an amazing range of personal experience to express it to me.

Rose was born in the Dakota Territory to Laura and Almanzo Wilder (her mother's books are familiar to millions and are the basis for the TV series "Little House on the Prairie"). Rose lived to be a Vietnam War correspondent for *Woman's Day* (to the great distress of the U.S. Defense Department). She had been a theoretical communist when young. But she saw the fallacies of collectivism after war-correspondent visits to the fledgling Soviet Union and elsewhere. For the rest of her life Rose was a powerful defender of the idea of the American Libertarian Revolution for freedom.

I used to hitchhike to her house during my school years, and learned much more from Rose than from any of my teachers. Later, as my career progressed, she made me her lawyer and business manager; still later, over my demurral, she made me executor to her estate, entrusted to carry out the many responsibilities she had accumulated in her extraordinary life. Rose died in her sleep in her beloved home in Danbury in late 1968, nearing 82 years of age.

Most of all, this book is for her.

Table of Contents

A New Dawn
For America:
The Libertarian Challenge

Introduction

Several times I've thought I might also have dedicated this book to "Toto" in honor of Dorothy's little dog, who unveiled the wizard as a humbug when humans were fooled.

No doubt you remember that delightful scene in the classic Judy Garland *Wizard of Oz* film. Dorothy and her companions return to the Emerald City for the favors the wizard has promised them. When the wizard appears, they are awed by his huge image, wreathed in belches of smoke and speaking in a great booming voice. But Toto is not fooled. Behind a screen he finds an ordinary little man operating a contraption that creates the whole illusion. There is no wizard!

"You're a very bad man," Dorothy says angrily when the truth is revealed. "Oh no, my dear," he replies, "I am a very good man. I'm just a very bad wizard." Then he shows the Tin Woodsman, the Scarecrow and the

Cowardly Lion that the heart and wisdom and courage they sought were within them all along.

*   *   *

Government is humbug. There is no government. Behind the noisy, smoke-belching, larger-than-life illusion of government are ordinary human beings. It isn't accurate to say government "is composed of" people; government *is* simply people. They may be good people but they are very bad wizards. Mortals have no magic.

Individuals are the only human reality. All groups are fictions. That is, groups have no concrete existence; they are not beings or entities in themselves; they exist only in the abstract, in the mind. Governments, nations, societies, classes, tribes, cub scout packs, football teams, corporations, labor unions, proletariats, political parties, majorities, elite minorities, communities, civilizations and such are all fictions. Those words only describe, or try to describe, a relationship between persons. Nothing new or superior is created by the use of such terms, for obviously one hundred heads together do not make one Great Head.

Individuals are the only reality. Groups have no body and soul, no rights and responsibilities. Groups cannot think, breathe, sleep, eat or drink. Groups cannot act morally or immorally; they can't act at all. Only individual humans have body and soul, duties and human rights. Only individuals are capable of moral or immoral behavior.

Every individual is unique. No two humans are identical *in any respect whatever*. No two have identical looks, backgrounds, personality. No two have the same set of values. No two have exactly the same goals in life. No two are exactly alike in mind or body—not just finger-prints, but cells, blood, bone, tissue, organs. No two react in the same way to food, medicines, stress, or to other human beings. All individuals pursue their own unique ends in their own unique way.

Humans are equal only in their humanness. We are all purposeful, volitional, independent beings. We are all, by our nature, free.

Liberty means the absence of forcible restraints. But freedom is one's control over one's own life-energy. Our self-control is inborn and unalienable. Others can, by force, thwart or curtail our freedom, but they can-not control us: they can't make our minds work or our muscles move, no matter *what* they do. Torture may persuade us to give information, for example, but it cannot actually in fact *make* our throats produce sound. In other words we are wholly self-controlling, self-responsible beings. We govern ourselves. "Govern-ment" by external force is literally impossible.

The instrument of our self-control is choice. The choices we make fulfill our purposes in life. We choose our course continuously according to our own unique circumstances, with every moment a new beginning. This page of this book will turn only if you *choose* to turn it. That's so even if you contrarily believe, as many profess to, that men are but helpless pawns shaped by their environment. The truth is rather that we shape our environment to make it congenial to our purposes,

3

when we are not prevented by physical fact or armed force. We arrange the furniture in our house and in our mind; we are not "arranged" by it.

Of course we are affected by our environment. We get what we need and want from the external world by attacking it with our life-energy directed by our power of choice. When our choices are narrowed by force, our life-energy is restricted accordingly. We are the less well able to sustain our lives. The individual's life-energy is the only human energy that exists. When liberty dies, men begin to.

These are the facts of our condition on earth.

*   *   *

America is the only country ever built on the truth of human freedom.

Always before—and *still* in all of the about forty countries I've visited—men and women believed their lives were controlled by an external Authority—by their Gods, by their Tribe, by their King, by their Parliament, by their President. Surprise! Those who articulated this idea divided people into the castes of rulers and the ruled, the few living in splendor off the toil of the many. The multitudes in the world, their ambitions silenced and their labor confiscated, have ever lived in darkness and squalor beyond our American imagining.

Early Americans learned the truth struggling for survival in a hard wilderness far from the power of English Authority. They grasped somehow that they were free, that *no* Authority controlled them. They had brought the idea of "government" with them, but five generations of frontier experience proved it false. Men controlled their own life-energy; to stay alive, they had to be free of restrictions on that energy.

In time Americans proclaimed as self-evident a truth taught by that struggle: that all men are endowed by the Creator of the universe with the unalienable rights of life and freedom. The hand of force, said Thomas Jefferson, may destroy, but cannot disjoin them.

The truth released a burst of creative human energy such as the world had never known, and created the modern world. The American Libertarian Revolution swept away absolutist regimes and beehive societies of much of the European world, teaching freedom.

But truths won by thought and effort may in time be gradually eclipsed. European Authorities —Kings and Presidents—gradually recaptured their subjects and power. And the time came when Americans began to be, stage by stage, convinced that maybe "government" really did have mystical powers.

Of course, only the forms of liberty are observed here now, without substance. Americans' life-energy is curtailed, regulated and confiscated by government. Most Americans in this decade have known nothing but what I must describe as submission to state servitude. They think they are free and they want to be free; but they are subtly deluded. They absent-mindedly believe in the wizard of Washington, and forget that wisdom and courage, energy and enterprise, lie within themselves. Let us therefore pull back the screen and scan what that wizard has accomplished.

"[Government in America] has taken on a vast mass of new duties and responsibilities; it has spread out its powers until they penetrate to every act of the citizen, however secret; it has begun to throw around its operations the high dignity and impeccability of a religion; its agents become a separate and superior caste, with authority to bind and loose, and their thumbs in every pot. But it still remains, as it was in the beginning, the common enemy of all well-disposed, industrious and decent men."

—H. L. Mencken

"No man's life, liberty or property are safe while the legislature is in session."

— New York State Surrogate Court Judge (Tucker 248, 1866)

1

Emergence of the American Superstate

The matter that most concerns libertarians today is the unchecked, malignant growth of the national "government" at Washington. In 1776, Americans denied old world Authority and began life free. Today power over our lives has largely passed from ourselves into the hands of government. Exactly this shift of power, from the individual to the State, has been the death sentence for every civilization before us.

What hope we have of averting the same fate for America lies in knowing the nature of our enemy: the Authority in Washington, D.C. Its activities are strikingly similar to those of the Roman Emperors fifteen centuries ago.

This is not what our forefathers bargained for. The founders thought they had fashioned a *new* form of government in this country, one reflecting the personal sovereignty of each individual in the United States and sharply limited in its reach. For a long time it seemed that our unique experiment had succeeded. Even into this century an American citizen could go about conducting his business without hindrance, cross the border without a passport, speak, dress, work, smoke, drink, skip school, maintain privacy, drive a vehicle without a license (much less a seat belt), and dress down any officious constable who questioned him. The national government had *no* power to tax his income or estate, nor could it steal his wealth with unredeemable paper money.

All this freedom is lost, of course. The trouble is, there are many Americans who don't know it. They go on thinking the government is the same as always; too large and wasteful, perhaps, but still "ours" and still, on the whole, benign. They go on indulging its expensive bumbling and meddling as a parent indulges a child. They grumble, but accept its claimed Authority. This attitude has been endlessly useful to Washington for expanding its power, picking our pockets and running our lives.

We can indulge no more. The American superstate at Washington is an established fact. What is important *now* is the need to recognize its destructive character and strip away its power to do harm.

The ancient origins of every State in the world but ours define their purposes to this day: they invariably originated in conquest, and have always existed for no other purpose than the economic exploitation of the

10

vanquished by the victors. They started in the dusty past when some nameless raider first spared his victim in order to enslave him. As the communities (*commune*-ities) thus created came into existence a uniform "political" attitude came into being. They became what we now call "nations", and as these "nations" devoured one another to become Empires, States became steadily more complex. But they never lost their character as an explicit instrument of exploitation. They existed, and exist today, as a mechanism for letting one group of people live off the toil of another. Today we talk of this as "redistribution of income": and that is the clue that now, after two centuries, the great experiment of Jefferson and Madison has come to naught. Washington, D.C. is like all the rest.

Washington is *not* touched by the supernatural. It is not a "transcendent being"; it is not omnipotent, nor eternal, nor ordained by God. It's just people, quite like anyone else: no more wise or high-minded, nor more stupid and dishonest.

What these ordinary people do *as goverment,* however, sets them very much apart from the rest of humanity: They make wars: Vietnam, Korea. They systematically rob the rest of the country: taxes, inflation,—and do it wholesale. They manufacture and sell privilege: tariffs on shoes, leases on Washington-owned land. They make rules without end: OSHA, the Federal Trade Commission—compelling everyone to do this and never that; but they often ignore these rule themselves. There seems to be no activity too dishonest, unjust, vicious, fraudu-

11

lent, stupid or criminal for many of them to pass up, as we have abundantly seen in recent years. If a citizen protests or resists their dictates, they make a satisfactory amount of trouble for him.

More ominous yet, the whole process of increasing Washington intervention is, like a drug habit, self-perpetuating and self-worsening. Each time it intervenes to deal with one problem, it breeds a new problem in some other, perhaps, unexpected, area.[1] (When somebody gets something for nothing, somebody gets nothing for something.) Politicians, who know exactly what is going on, then come forward to suggest further State interventions to deal with the new problems, and so on and on.

As de Lawd remarked in *The Green Pastures*, when you have passed a miracle, you have to pass another one to take care of the first. In the process, for most of us the economic situation grows slowly but certainly worse, and our options fewer.

Washington's habit of shipping every imaginable social and economic problem to Uncle Sam has cost us

1. For one example (among hundreds), consider minimum wage laws, which cause unemployment among marginal workers, notably young people, especially minorities. The first intervention, the minimum wage, does not of course create any new wealth to pay the workers with; so its effect is to redistribute the existing wage pool. Some workers get more, while some whose services are worth less to an employer than the legal minimum will find themselves out of a job, or unable to find a job. At this point the President and Congress suggest new interventions, such as job training for the workers they have cheated, or more police to deal with the idled and angry young people on the streets.

dearly. Unimaginable sums, literally trillions of dollars, have been confiscated and spent for social doctoring, and it is difficult to find any area of life that has not been *worsened* as a result. Greater than the waste of money is the price we have paid in freedom lost, dreams indefinitely delayed, opportunities missed, and the doom ordained for building our house upon the sands of false belief.

All we have to show for this heartbreaking mistake is more taxes, more bureaucrats and more problems. Blind to the exploitive character of Washington, you and I fall into the trap of supposing that *it* wants a "good society" the way *we* want a "good society." It does not; it wants power and more power. The politicians' adventures in social action are but a means to the historical end, a pretense for adding on more layers of bureaucracy and taxes and power over us. Were they actually to succeed, in winning the "War against Poverty" for instance, it would put legions of poverty-fighting bureaucrats out of work (in a typical federal anti-poverty program, over three-quarters of the funds go to pay federal salaries and administrative costs, while only the small balance gets to the intended beneficiaries, the politically defined poor). It would also lose control over a lot of its dependents — and freeing slaves has never been a popular pastime.

It is no coincidence that nearly all of the urging of Washington—and each state government—toward "social action" comes from the exploiters themselves—from politicians and their larcenous allies, the interest groups. They know perfectly well what they are doing. They expect, with ample reason, to redistribute some of our money to themselves. Open any newspaper any day and you can read two stories about the failure of some government social enterprise, and three stories about politicians asking for new powers to do even more for us.

Bureaucrats need never fear losing their jobs by solving social problems. Even if they wanted to—and obviously there are very many who do—they would be thwarted by bedrock principles.

Washington's primary functions are those that require the use of force and compulsion: national defense and protection of individual rights. Indeed, the only tasks it can perform competently are those requiring police methods.

But for ironclad reasons, the use of force and compulsion are completely unsuitable for social and economic purposes. Compulsion cannot grow our food or build our houses. We wouldn't hire policemen to straighten our teeth or fix the television set. But the strange thing is, that is exactly what the politicians have increasingly done for sixty years and more. They've asked for more police headquarters to educate our children, to run the airlines and railroads, rebuild slums, manage television and radio communications, protect the environment, prevent discrimination, and to undertake countless other nonpolice chores they manifestly cannot do adequately, or at all.

"It is a curious anomaly," the great libertarian Albert J. Nock wrote. "State power has an unbroken record of inability to do anything efficiently, economically, disinterestedly or honestly; yet when the slightest dissatisfaction arises over any exercise of social power, the aid of the agent least qualified to give aid is immediately called for." But called for by whom, and why?

The direct cost of State intervention is measurable in dollars and cents. According to the Tax Foundation, the current price of government at all levels is *$7,792 per household per year.* Is it worth $150 a week to you to be "governed"?

The indirect cost is undoubtedly greater. The progressive confiscations of Washington deter productivity: we lose what might have been. You and I lose new technology, new inventions, new medicines that may be a matter of life and death to us. You and I lose job opportunities, freedom of action, chances of betterment. You and I lose control of our future, for in the end Washington tries to determine our very means of survival.

Any superstate such as Washington must become antisocial in character. Rather than encourage the normal and healthy growth of social power, it has, as President James Madison observed, an innate "lust to expand" *its* power, with an appetite that grows with every bite.

The question now is how far are we down "the well-traveled road to absolutism"? How much time do we have left to do something about it?

Consider the following facts: Washington has increased *one-hundredfold* in size and power in just the last forty-five years; government at all levels continues to double every seven years, while the economic energy

15

that sustains our lives grows much more slowly, doubling every thirty years. Washington and state government confiscations in the period have jumped from less than a tenth to nearly half your income, so that if you are an average person you pay more in taxes than you do for all the necessities of life put together—food, clothing, shelter and medicine. More than all of that in *taxes!*

If present trends continue, the absorption of resources by Washington will likely cause complete national financial collapse *within ten years.* So implies 1974 Nobel Prize winning economist Friedrich von Hayek, a libertarian; certainly New York City's debacle has shown the way.

I remain optimistic that we can pull out of this mess. I think so because America's circumstances are to some degree unique in history. In this country liberty got a head start on the State to an extent never before achieved. Though freedom wanes, its traditions are still ingrained in the American character. I think they will inspire the imagination of this generation. Americans have this—perhaps next to last—chance to recognize Washington for what it now is and strip it of its power to harm. Even those Americans who *are* the State may see the whole truth and abandon its cause in favor of old-fashioned American freedom. May a good job and a clear conscience await any bureaucrat who quits!

"The so-called American capitalist, today, usually does not know what genuine free enterprise is. It means the total exclusion of the state from the economic realm, leaving producers free to compete, subject to the risks and hazards of the law of supply and demand alone. But the contemporary businessman's working definition of 'free enterprise' is bribing specific government officials for favors—for contracts, for subsidies, for monopolies, for protective tariffs . . . for shelter *against* competition at home and abroad."

—Edith Efron

"Government is the only agency that can take a useful commodity like paper, slap some ink on it, and make it totally worthless."

—Ludwig von Mises

2

The American Economy

This country is in an economic mess. That fact is admitted by liberals and conservatives, Democrats and Republicans alike.

Taxes everywhere are so high that they are visibly crippling enterprise, saving, investment, and productive activity. Throughout the country people are rebelling against extortionate income taxes, inheritance taxes, property taxes, sales taxes, and countless "nuisance" taxes in every walk of life.

Government budgets and their debts at all levels are rising out of control. Cities like New York, suffering from vast and swollen expenditures, teeter on the edge of outright bankruptcy, and state governments are not far behind. Bankruptcies plague sector after sector of the private economy.

The high rate of unemployment has been a particularly painful recent phenomenon in most of America. It is unpleasantly accompanied by a jamming of the welfare rolls, increasing a burden on that part of the economy still productively at work.

As if all this were not enough, our number one economic problem is still with us and getting worse: chronic, escalating inflation. For the past two decades, the annual rate of inflation has been steadily accelerating and in 1973-74 reached the frightening and unprecedented annual rate of 14 percent. Inflation is debasing the dollar, wiping out the value of savings, crippling the real income and the standard of living of the average American, and destroying valid business calculation of profits and losses. Often these days businesses congratulate themselves on their high level of profits, and left-wing critics attack their "swollen" nature. But both groups ignore the fact that the profits are illusory products of inflation. They disregard the fact that much of the profits are needed simply to replace higher-priced machinery and inventory, and thus are not "profits" at all, but merely funds needed to maintain the business. The illusions of inflationary accounting are encouraged by the fact that government forces businesses to keep their books in this fashion, and it taxes business as if these profits were real.

The fact that the *rate* of inflation fell off during 1975 is cold comfort. For since the autumn of 1973 we have been in the midst of the most severe recession (actually a depression) since the Great Depression of the 1930s. Industrial production and the output of the economy have been falling, and unemployment at its height rose to nearly 10 percent. In previous recessions and depressions prices have always declined, so that the average consumer could at least enjoy a drop in his cost of living and recoup some of the losses in real income suffered during the preceding inflationary boom. But now, for the first time in American history, consumer prices have continued to rise—and rise substantially—even during a depression.

This mess has come about after forty years of "fine-tuning" the economy by government planners and Establishment economists. For forty years, these men have assured us that the boom-bust cycle was a thing of the past, that by wise adjustment of government taxes and expenditures, we would no longer suffer either inflations, booms, or recessions. Government planning and intervention had supposedly stepped in to "save capitalism". Yet, now, after 40 years of such allegedly wise forecasting and fine-tuning, using the most up-to-date electronic computers, our rulers have only succeeded in plunging us into *both* a boom *and* a bust *at the same time*. Promising grandly to save us from either inflation or depression, they have only succeeded in bringing us both at once.

Our Establishment politicians and economists are in despair, and no wonder. Their theories have proved worthless; they can only go back to the futile pushing of the same old, discredited buttons. But they can't keep doing the same old things, because they are caught in a trap where the old buttons, the old measures, cannot possibly work. If the government spends more, increases the money supply, incurs more deficits, it *might* cure the depression, but only at the price of a far greater and accelerated inflation next year, and of suffering *more severe* depression and unemployment later on.

It is obvious we have reached such a deep and pervasive economic crisis that piddling, piecemeal reforms will no longer help much, even in the short-run. There must be a drastic change in economic policy in order to help, to get us out of the crises. So it's "back to the old drawing board." But back to *what*?

Some Establishment figures—businessmen, politicians, economists, labor leaders—are calling for the scrapping of our private enterprise system altogether and for full-scale collectivist economic planning. But it should be clear by now that (apart from the despotism and massive coercion of such a scheme) this won't work either. All forms of collectivist central planning have been tried during our century: socialism, Communism, fascism, corporate-statism—and all of these have failed, and failed dismally. The central economic planning of the Hitler regime in the 1930s and 40s ruined Germany, which only escaped and regained its prosperity (in the Western part) by removing government controls and returning to a largely free economy in 1948. Communist planning, despite its use of massive coercion, hasn't worked either. It's surprising but true that the Communist countries of Eastern Europe have begun to move away from planning and toward a free-market economy. In England, we have the devastating spectacle of a country brought to its economic knees by decades of socialist policy.

And so, the dream of collectivism is no longer fresh and new—it is the same tired old stuff, which creates a nightmare existence for the population as well as economic impoverishment and despair.

No, what our economy suffers from is not a lack of government intervention and activity but far too much; the route back to prosperity and economic sanity is the road *away* from collectivism and toward freedom. Not only is a free market economy liberated from government intervention the only *moral* solution for America and the rest of the world; it is also the only *practical* way of restoring economic health and prosperity. We not only should have a radical turn toward freedom and a free economy; we *must* have it in order to survive, grow and prosper.

Let us take the crucial problem of inflation, a malady that has plagued the world, again and again, for many centuries. For all those centuries, governments and their spokesmen have blamed many groups in society for causing inflation: sometimes all at once, other times in rapid succession. Consumers are blamed for spending "too much", for being "piggish". Apparently, a sudden onset of piggishness among the public is supposed to be the fatal cause of inflation. Liberals tend to blame business "monopoly" for inflation: wicked and "greedy" businessmen decide to raise prices in order to increase their profits. Conservatives like to blame greedy labor unions for demanding higher wage rates and thereby pushing prices up.

But there are deep and crucial flaws in all of these arguments. As for the consumers, why would they suddenly become "piggish", and why in the world should their piggishness increase every year? More to the point, where do they get the *money* to fuel their increasing spending? How do they pay for it? As for businessmen, if they had the "monopoly" power to raise prices, why didn't they do so a long time ago? Why do they raise prices by a certain percentage each year, and not grab everything at once? In short, what *limits* them from raising prices still further? The same point applies to unions. If unions are that powerful, why don't they grab all their wage increases at once? Why limit their demands to a certain percentage raise per year?

The fact is that all these groups are severely limited in the amount they can spend or charge in prices. Consumers are limited in spending by their income, by the amount of *money* they have available. Businessmen are limited in the prices they can charge by the amount of *money* the consumers are willing to spend, which in turn is limited by the quantity of money they have. Union demands are limited by the amount of *money* the employers can pay, which in turn is limited by the quantity of money the consumers have to spend. We see, then, that the chief factor in the whole affair is how much money the consumers have, which in turn is determined by *how much money exists* in the economy.

The key to the whole problem, then, is the supply of money in the economy. Who determines that quantity of money? Not the consumers, businessmen or unions; none of these groups has the power to create money. If any of them tried to print money, they would go very rapidly to jail for the high crime of counterfeiting. The answer is that there is only one organization in society that has the power, and the absolute power at that, to create money: the federal government. The government in short, has the legal monopoly of counterfeiting, which is handled specifically by the Federal Reserve Bank.

It was not always thus. Originally, before the galloping march of statism in the twentieth century, money developed as a useful commodity, produced and exchanged on the free market. Money was that commodity, generally (but not invariably) gold or silver, which the market decided was most useful in serving that purpose. Its quantity was regulated by the demands of the free marketplace. Gold and silver are rare enough metals to be very costly to mine and produce, and so these metals retain their value over long periods of time. Money creation, and hence inflation, became rare and difficult.

In the nineteenth century, for example, the "dollar" was defined as one-twentieth of a gold ounce. That's what a "dollar" *was*. And all the other major world currencies: the pound, the franc, the mark, etc., were also units of weight of gold. But during the onrushing statism of the twentieth century, all governments, including the federal government of the United States, have seized control of the money-creating apparatus. Gold has been shoved into the dim background, and the "dollar" and other currencies are now names for mere pieces of paper, paper which can be and is created at will by the government printing press, the Federal Reserve System.

Why did they seize control? The answer should be obvious. Who *wouldn't* want to grab control of the power to print money, to finance one's deficits and expenditures, and to lend or give away to favored political groups? That is precisely what the U.S. government has been doing. Every year, every month, every week, the Federal Reserve creates more money, and uses that money to finance government deficits and to lend out at cheap rates to favored groups. And as the government pumps ever more of the new money into the economy, as the new money ripples out into society, consumers spend it and prices inexorably go up.

In former times, as in the case of the American "continentals" during the Revolution, or the "greenbacks" during the Civil War, it was easy for the public to understand the inflationary process. The federal government pumped new paper money into the system, prices rose, and the value of that money fell in relation to goods and services and in relation to gold. But today money-creation is accomplished through absolute Federal Reserve control of the nation's banking system, so that most of the inflation takes place through the creation, the "printing", of new bank deposits engineered by the Fed. But how many people understand the banking process? And so, week after week, the Fed creates new bank dollars and paper dollars, prices rise, the public doesn't understand the obscure process, and the government can get off the hook by loudly blaming those scapegoat groups for the inflation: businesses, unions, or consumers. But the real culprit is the federal government, which keeps on its merry way inflating the money supply and driving prices upward.

Let us turn for a moment to a related question: what is responsible for the familiar boom-bust cycle, that cycle which has now brought us the cruel dilemmas of the inflationary depression? For four decades, we have been told by our rulers that the boom-bust cycle is caused by processes deep within the free market economy, and that wise Washington economic doctors must cure the cycle by fine-tune planning: by pumping money and deficits into the economy during a recession, and by taking money out (usually by higher taxes) during an inflationary boom. But once again, the culprit in the event of recession is not any inherent market deficiency of consumers or investors. The fatal flaw is the government's favorite policy of inflating the supply of money and credit.

When the Federal Reserve and its controlled banking system inflates the money supply by lending newly created bank deposits to businessmen (one of the typical processes of inflation), the result is not only an increase in prices. Even more hidden and unwelcome processes are launched by this expansion of credit. For businesses now receive newly inflated money at a cheap price, at an interest rate below the free-market level, simply because an increase in the supply of any commodity tends to lower its unit price.

27

This new and inexpensive credit stimulates unsound investments in capital goods: construction, buildings and machines, inventory, etc. Investments in lengthy and time-consuming projects which previously looked unprofitable now seem profitable because of the fall in the interest charge. Too many resources (workers, savings, capital funds) are invested in these "capital goods" industries, and not enough are invested in producing goods and services directly for consumers. In short, there is an "overinvestment" or "malinvestment" in the capital goods industries such as buildings, machine tools, and industrial raw materials. We can say that business is fooled by the cheap credit into thinking that the consumers wish to save more and to consume less than they really do.

On the free market, when businesses make such a systematic mistake, the new money is paid out by the capital goods industries to the workers in those industries. Then the workers move to reestablish their preferred proportion of consumption and saving: to consume more, and to save and invest less, than the businessmen expect. The result is that the "malinvestment"—the unsound over-investment in capital goods—is quickly liquidated, idled employees and resources flow back into consumer goods' production in the proper proportions, and the economy has fully recovered. We see now that this "recession" in capital goods industries is the healthy and necessary process by which the market liquidates unsound investments, and returns the economy to good health and sound and efficient production to meet consumer demands.

Left to itself, the boom and the "recession" of unsound capital investments would be very brief and almost unnoticed. Why is it then that the inflationary boom generally goes on for years and leads to a painful and visible recession? The answer is that the whole process would be brief and unnoticed, *if* the injection of new inflationary credit were only a small, one-shot affair. But what happens is that the government keeps the inflation going, continues to pump in new bank loans to business, and thereby keeps the process going one step ahead of retribution. And the longer the process continues, the greater will be the magnitude of the unsound investments, and the more painful and longer will be the recession or depression in the capital goods industries.

The crunch arrives when it becomes apparent to the government that once the inflationary bank credit stops growing, the inevitable recession *must* ensue. Furthermore, the longer the inflation proceeds, the greater the rate at which the government must pump in new money to solve business's "liquidity crunch", to try to avoid the inevitable corrective process of the ever-more menacing recession. The government truly has a tiger by the tail. It is very much like the process of drug addiction. The longer the addiction proceeds, the greater and more rapid must be the new doses of the drug to keep up one's "kicks" and to avoid the ever more painful withdrawal symptoms.

But just as the addiction *must* eventually stop to avoid

the death of the addict, so the inflationary increase of money *must* cease, otherwise the economy will suffer the fantastic runaway inflation that afflicted Germany in 1923, and many other countries since. If we keep on our current collision course, we will see the day when $1 trillion will be needed to buy a loaf of bread; and, after that, we will still suffer the depression needed to reestablish economic recovery.

And so it is hopelessly self-defeating to try to avoid the pitfalls of recession by inflating the money supply still further. Most of us will be wiped out by accelerating inflation still more until it runs away into the stratosphere, only making the ensuing corrective depression even more painful. In any case, *if* the government doesn't intervene in a recession or depression to try to stop the processes of adjustment, to try to prop up the unsound investments or keep up prices or wage rates, the processes of recession are almost always over quickly. Nineteenth-century business-cycle recessions, unhampered by government intervention, rarely lasted longer than a year and a half. Hardly had they begun when they were over and sound prosperity was resumed.

The cure for any depression, then, is the same as the cure for our galloping inflation, and it is a simple one: *the federal government must stop inflating the money supply.* If the government ceased and desisted from printing or creating new money, the inflation would stop short and the recession would be over in a very brief period of time. The government must also avoid interfering with the recession process by keeping up unsound investments, prices, or wage rates.

There is, however, one thing that the government *can* do to speed up the recession-adjustment process. And, fortunately, this measure will also aid the long-range prosperity of the country. The government can drastically cut its own budget, its taxes and expenditures. This would lift the great and crippling burden of taxes from the backs of our producers and workers. It would allow people to save and spend their own money in whatever ways they saw fit. But, what is more, the cut in taxes would allow more savings and thereby render economically useful some of the previously unsound investments. The recession would be over that much faster.

We see then that the first, and immediate, thing that the federal government must do is to *stop creating new money:* to stop "inflating". This it can do in the present economy if the Federal Reserve (a) never again lowers bank reserve requirements; and (b) never again purchases any assets (for this is the major method by which the Fed creates new bank reserves and new money). These are the necessary immediate reforms. But ultimately it is imperative to *take away* the power of the federal government to create new money; for if we leave any group with the power to counterfeit, that power will be used. We must do away with the central bank of our day (as President Andrew Jackson did away with his) altogether. This country grew and prospered very well before the creation of the Federal Reserve System in 1913, and we can do so again. And

31

we must end the power of the government to create "dollars" at will; money must once again be a commodity such as gold, produced solely on the free market.

As we have seen, these measures would end the boom-bust cycle as well as inflation, but we can speed up the adjustment to recession, and grow and prosper far more if we cut taxation and government expenditures drastically. It is particularly important to work toward early repeal of the income tax. This tax is not only the major tax instrument in the country, and not only a grave crippler of saving and investment, but also the leading method by which the government pries into every aspect of our daily lives, into our activities, expenditures, and bank accounts. Again, this country got along very well before 1914 without income taxation.

Pending its elimination, it is vital that we repeal the withholding provision of the income tax, a measure that arrived as late as World War II, supposedly as a wartime "emergency" measure. Without the slyly facile system of withholding, it would be impossible for the government to collect the present confiscatory tax rates from each citizen. Government would then *have* to reduce its swollen level of taxation and spending.

And pending the repeal of all taxes on income and capital gains, we should remove such inequities as the corporate income tax (which imposes a double tax on stockholders who also pay on their dividend) and eliminate ways in which inflation creates a whipsaw effect by also automatically increasing taxation. Thus, inflation may cause a person's salary to double from

$6,000 to $12,000; prices may have doubled so that his "real income" or standard of living may be the same, and yet because of the "progressive" feature of the income tax, his tax burden will be considerably higher than before. Also, capital "gains" may be illusory because of inflation; certainly, the illusory gains, just as in the case of illusory profits, should not be subject to tax.

On the local level, it is important to reduce greatly the crippling and growing burden of property taxes. New York City and other municipalities must not be allowed to attempt to solve the problems created by their reckless budgets by imposing more taxes on a long suffering public; they must cut their expenditures, and cut them steeply. Eventually, of course, we will want to look into the feasibility of creating a truly voluntaristic society in which *all* goods and services are provided on the free market.

Contrary to the propaganda of expedience, there is no real conflict between the demands of moral principle and of pragmatic reality. There is no real conflict between the moral principles of individual liberty and private property on the one hand, and the requirements of economic health and prosperity on the other. *Both* require getting government out of our lives and out of our pockets.

To restore economic health, we must drastically reduce government budgets, corporate bailouts, subsidies, taxes, controls, and regulations; and we must separate the money supply from the State as we have previously separated religion from the government. The prescription for our economic ills is the same as for our moral ills: to slash state power and to allow individual freedom and private property rights to prevail.

"To be governed is to be watched, inspected, spied upon, directed, law-ridden, regulated, penned up, indoctrinated, preached at, checked, appraised, seized, censured, commanded, by beings who have neither title, nor knowledge, nor virtue. To be governed is to have every movement noted, registered, counted, rated, stamped, measured, numbered, assessed, licensed, refused, authorized, endorsed, admonished, prevented, reformed, redressed, corrected."

—P. J. Proudhon, 1849

"Were we directed from Washington when to sow, and when to reap, we should soon want bread."

—Thomas Jefferson

3

Politicizing America

Scarcely a single aspect of our lives remains in which the government has not hindered the productive supply of goods and services we need. Or made that supply not only more expensive, but often of a much lower quality than otherwise would be the case. Let's look at a few areas that touch us every day.

The U.S. Postal Service

This giant government-owned monopoly corporation has been going from bad to worse over the last couple of decades, until now it ranks as the single most criticized commercial institution in the United States. It not only doesn't deliver the mail on time, but sometimes doesn't deliver it at all. And it performs that service at a first class letter rate—as I write—of 13¢, a gigantic rip-off. Analytical studies have shown that the actual cost of handling a first class letter is approximately 8¢, and that the additional 5¢ you pay goes to subsidize other classes of mail. Does it make sense for you to support giant publishing corporations like Time, Inc. to deliver magazines to others, and contribute to mail-order firms so they may choke our boxes with catalogs?

Study after study has indicated where the trouble lies: the post office has a monopoly on first class mail, and hence there is no competitive pressure to improve service. Further, as a "non-profit corporation" there is no incentive to do better, and no measure of market performance. In point of fact the post office loses high in the hundreds of millions of dollars each year, which comes out of your pockets and mine in the form of appropriated tax money.

The answer of course is to place the movement of mail in the private sector of the economy where it belongs. At the very least, Congress ought to repeal all laws prohibiting competition to the Postal Service and inhibiting entry into the field. Of course that wouldn't wholly solve the problem as Congress would doubtless appropriate ever larger sums to keep a withering post office in business. Hence a Libertarian administration would move immediately to convert the Postal Service into an operation for profit, and sell shares of stock in it (carrying title to all its assets such as post offices and delivery trucks) to investors across America. Owing to its present state of decline, I'd guess the price per share would be less than it might be, but on the other hand with heads-up management appointed by a return-oriented ownership, this sleeping giant might just be able to take advantage of its present market dominance to keep ahead of competitors. In any event, all of us consumers would be pretty well assured of a return to a 6 or 7 ¢ stamp to move letters promptly.

Transportation

Let's look at moving things—you, and anything you want to ship, or buy. The federal government has managed to snarl this area of our lives beyond belief.

Begin with your car. Since 1968 the federal government has required that a great number of devices be added to your car, in the name of your safety or even to deter theft. They range from heavy bumpers to ignition locking and buzzing systems. Some of these you might want; some of them you would not want. The dollar cost of these items, all required—you must have them whether you choose or not—is now nearly $500 per car. That's in addition to the kind of car with normal safety and protection features you could have bought in 1967. Of course, your operating costs are also measurably higher owing to the added weight and complexity of the mandated features—and gallons per mile are up.

On top of that, if you choose to buy a foreign car there is a tariff which you must pay. If you're buying a

Mercedes, you will pay to the federal treasury from $198 to $537 for the privilege. If you're buying a much less expensive car, the Volkswagen, the tariff you must pay ranges from $112 to $153, depending on the model and price. Since you're getting the same federally required whether-you-want-them-or-not features in these cars as in General Motors or Fords, the total cost to you, *on top of* what the maker would be glad to sell you as transportation, could run to $1,037 for the Mercedes and $653 for the Volkswagen.

Suppose you want to fly from New York to California. You must fly that route on air carriers which were servicing that route when the Civil Aeronautics Board was established back in the 1930s or which are mergers or extensions of carriers then in existence. There haven't been any major new interstate air carriers to come into being in the United States in 40 years! Competition has been frozen, and frozen because the CAB wants it that way—and so do the airlines now in existence.

In 1975 the President of World Airways applied for permission to transport passengers for $89 per person coast to coast—about one-half of the fare established by the CAB for the major airlines. World Airways is a very large charter airline with an admirable safety record, upheld even during the last days of Viet Nam when it ferried enormous numbers of refugees out of Viet Nam under harrowing conditions. Early in 1976 the CAB rejected the World request, as it has rejected so many analogous applications. You therefore may continue to fly from New York to California on one of

40

the airlines protected from price competition, happy in the knowledge that the stockholders of TWA are blessing and thanking you.

Or would you prefer to travel on the railway? Amtrak is a government-created corporation fed hundreds of millions of dollars a year in tax money in order to provide you with very dubious passenger service at a high price on various of the nation's railways. For $120 you can ride for 37 hours from Chicago to St. Petersburg, Florida. But it costs Amtrak $384 to take you; it would be *cheaper* for the government to give you first class airfare and $100 to spend at the beach! But the *Floridian* rolls on.

The railroads are happy with this situation because they no longer are in the business of carrying passengers. They found *that* too costly owing to rulings by the Interstate Commerce Commission making it impossible to charge market rates for transportation, owing to refusal of that Commission to let them discontinue disused and unprofitable lines, owing to subsidization by the federal government (with taxpayer money) of other means of transportation in direct competition with the railroads.

Even without the passenger-service losses, a number of Northeastern railroads have gone bankrupt in the last few years. Now Congress has created a monster called Conrail, a privately owned corporation taking over the assets of most of those railroads. The original plan was to infuse it with $1.9 billion of your tax money to get the operation going. Over the years, would you care to estimate how much more it will get from the federal treasury?

American shipping? Monopoly union legislation allows the most outrageous kind of feather-bedding to exist on what are called "American bottoms"; this, with U.S. rate-making laws, makes our ships internationally noncompetitive. To make up for *that* the Congress has provided that all military goods and at least half of other government goods be shipped in U.S. vessels. And "foreign bottoms" are forbidden to carry cargo between American ports. How much is all this costing us in wasted tax dollars and higher freight charges?

Clearly, the federal transportation "policy" is hideously and expensively wrong. We must set matters straight by removing government entirely from the field.

Paperwork

Perhaps the government does not yet have a monopoly on red tape, but they seem to be working on it. According to the office of Management and Budget in 1974 there were 5,146 different *types* of approved public-use forms (*not counting* tax and banking forms) required of business by the government. A New York firm employing less than fifty people in that year had to fill out 37 federal filings on 12 different forms, 26 sets of data for nine New York State agencies, and 25 forms for 12 city departments. Just one large corporation with about 40,000 employees, according to economist Murray L. Weidenbaum, must use 125 file drawers of backup material simply to meet federal reporting requirements on personnel—and that calls for the equivalent of 14 fulltime employees; its management indicated that one-third of its staff could be eliminated if there were no federal, state or local reporting requirements.

All in all, individuals in business firms spend over 130 million man hours a year filling out federal forms alone—according to the federal government itself! Imagine the cost of filling those out; imagine how much less each businessman could charge you and me for a product that didn't have to bear such a heavy unrelated cost. Time to begin a massive slashing in these requirements? To ask the question supplies the answer.

Social Security

Let's look at your "old age pension" as it is seductively described by the federal government: the Social Security benefits you are promised. I think now everyone understands that the Social Security system is a gigantic hoax. It resembles a pyramid. Those oldsters at the top receive funds only so long as an ever increasing number of young people enter at the bottom. Since those youngsters are being promised benefits only one-quarter of what they could obtain with the same funds invested in a private insurance plan, a question arises as to how long they will stand for it.

In the short run, as President Ford pointed out in his State of the Union address in 1976, the Social Security system faces a cash-flow problem: outlays exceed receipts. President Ford's solution (like that of everyone before him as this problem recurs) is to raise the payroll tax. But the roughly $45 billion in additional tax funds will be gone in four years unless the economy grows at *twice* its historic rate, which is the convenient assumption the administration made. And in connection with the politicians' short-run solution, let me in passing make the point that increasing taxes always makes the problem worse, not better, because doing so discourages production and diminishes the tax base.

The long run problem is actuarial balance: more benefits have already been promised than the economy can be expected to pay even with rapid growth. For the system to be in *theoretical* actuarial balance between presently promised benefits and present tax rates, the "trust fund" would have to be almost *50 times* as big as it is, or about 2.3 trillion dollars.

Incidentally, this huge unfunded liability is about five times larger than the government reported 'national debt' and should properly be included as a part of the total debt figure, though government officials conveniently ignore this fact. Also, it is not coincidental that job producing capital for American industry has become scarcer as the Social Security debt has grown larger. Individuals who, in a free society, would be providing for their own retirement by investing in stocks and bonds now presume (incorrectly) that the government has done that for them.

And, please note: the so-called "trust fund" consists not of real wealth of any kind, but merely of government bonds (promises to pay) in the vaults of the Social Security Administration. Payout depends upon collecting face value of a bond; the Administrator must ask the Department of the Treasury to cash it in. The Treasury can only pay by notifying Congress to appropriate some current tax money, or by creating new money to pay off. To say, then, that there is a trust fund of any meaningful nature is equivalent to saying that you may successfully climb a cobweb ladder.

Looking at the Social Security situation without rose-colored glasses, I can only reach the conclusion that it is, in the vernacular, busted. Payouts to those who are promised benefits depend entirely on the future willingness of those in government to raise taxes to pay the promised benefits. And how long can that go on? Remember New York City's pledge that its municipal bonds had first call on tax receipts?

Manifestly the situation is out of control, and countless millions of Americans are going to be cruelly disappointed after having been cruelly taxed for much of their lives. It is imperative that a humanitarian Libertarian administration avert disaster before it becomes impossible.

That can only be done by replacing the present system in its entirety. It is impossible to reform; there is nothing to reform. It was in the first place a tragic error for the government to presume to provide for the American people's retirement. Now there are no easy solutions. Few problems faced by this nation are as

45

serious or potentially explosive as the Social Security fraud. The longer the public is kept ignorant of the literal bankruptcy of the System the more dangerous the situation becomes.

Our objective must be to return to a system of private pensions, annuities and individual responsibility for one's own retirement years. Further, there can be no question but that the American people will willingly return to their traditional charitable generosity toward those unable to provide for themselves—once the government ceases robbing them of 40-50% of their earnings.

There are several steps that could be taken immediately to facilitate the transition to a private retirement system in America. To begin with we could end inflation (which hits hardest those dependent on fixed incomes) by following those steps outlined earlier in this book. Secondly, all persons over 55 years of age could be exempted from all taxation and all restrictions which place a ceiling on the earnings of older citizens. Next, younger people (say, those under 40) could be freed of the onerous Social Security payroll tax and encouraged to invest in private retirement plans. Such plans would in most cases provide for greater retirement benefits than are even promised by Social Security (and which cannot be fulfilled, anyway). For those between the ages of 40 and 55 a graduated system combining a reduction of both benefits and taxes could be implemented.

To help fund that portion of remaining benefits the United States government should undertake a systematic sale of all of its mammoth land and industrial holdings. Such a program, combined with the greatly increased productivity available from an economy freed of bureaucratic constraints, is eminently feasible. It is a humanitarian plan. It faces up to a problem which must be dealt with quickly if we are to avoid the catastrophic consequences of proceeding along the fraudulent path of the present Social Security System.

Life-aiding Drugs

How about drug safety? Surely *there* is an area in which the federal government through the Food and Drug Administration has saved us from terrible tragedies like that caused in Europe by thalidomide fifteen years ago. True?

Not true, says Professor Sam Peltzman of the University of Chicago in a massive and unrefuted study completed in 1974. After the thalidomide tragedy, "toughening" amendments were added to the existing Food and Drug Act, which he demonstrates have had the following effects: 1) The number of new drugs brought to the market each year has been cut by half with no corresponding reduction in inefficacious drugs; 2) The cost of drug development has doubled; 3) Drug prices have increased because of reduced competition among drugs—so that the sick yearly pay $50 million extra; and 4) Substantial net social costs have been incurred from deaths and illnesses that could have been prevented if the development of new

47

drugs had not been hampered by the amendments. Says Peltzman, "Consumer losses from purchases of ineffective drugs or hastily marketed unsafe drugs appear to have been trivial compared to the gains [formerly available] from innovation."

What this means could become ghastly clear to you. Suppose your doctor tells you you are dying from a form of cancer for which there is no known cure. He adds that there are experimental drugs being used in Italy and Japan which have in some cases prevented deaths of persons with problems like yours. You ask him to get a supply on the chance that it may work in your case. "Oh no," he says. "I cannot legally obtain the drugs in the United States, and if I could obtain them I could not legally prescribe them. The FDA requires a lengthy testing procedure before a new drug comes on the market. Perhaps in three or four years from now they may be available." "But you tell me I won't be alive in three or four years," you say. "That's true," he says, "but the law gives the Food and Drug Administration the authority to decide what's best for you and me." He reserves your space in the terminal illness section of the hospital ten months hence.

The FDA of course has extended its big brotherly hand even in the area of vitamin pill formulation. It used to be that you could buy from one pharmaceutical manufacturer or another a vitamin pill compounded to meet your own individual decision about the vitamins your body needs. This is no longer the case; the strength of certain vitamins, such as A, have been limited within each pill by the FDA. That means to get the combination you want you may have to dispense for yourself a number of different pills daily in order to make up your own formulation. A petty matter? Of course, but another indication that what you or your doctor may think best for you is allowed *only* if the bureaucrats in Washington agree.

Time for a change? Of course; a humanitarian Libertarian administration would sweep away the FDA and all its abuses, in favor of developing institutions in the private sector to pass upon the safety and efficacy of old and new drugs alike, much as the Consumer's Union now functions in other fields. Because pharmaceutical companies have an overwhelming interest in marketing safe drugs, and because of the natural caution of most physicians, the chance of a significant problem arising is extremely remote.

Corporation Coddling

It should come as a surprise to no one that Washington is deeply entangled in the business of granting special favors to influential and strategically positioned business leaders, corporations, and financial institutions. The result has been the gradual creation of two different types of business enterprise: those in what economist Walter Grinder calls the "protected sector" and those who rather than being aided are exploited in the "competitive sector".

The outstanding characteristic of the protected sector is that the industries involved are to a greater or lesser degree protected from competition by the Federal government, granted financial help by the government, and/or bailed out with tax money if the wolf arrives at the door.

There are tariffs and import quota systems to protect the makers of textiles, television sets—and General Motors.

There are "incredible love affairs going on between the regulators and the regulated", says a justice department's deputy assistant Attorney General for anti-trust. As a result the agencies often condone or even champion monopolistic practices and rubber-stamp higher prices for everything from airline tickets to telephone calls. Among the agencies with the worst reputation is the Interstate Commerce Commission, which protects the trucking industry from unwanted competition and rate lowering. But there are plenty of others like the Federal Maritime Commission and the rate-making Federal Power Commission.

There are the innumerable corporations who stay in business solely because they have wangled lucrative contracts with one agency or another of the government, extending across the board from the military to the "Foods for Peace" program.

When business enterprises falter owing to shifts in markets or just management incompetence, they usually become dinosaurs which ought to collapse. That process of course shifts capital to new and dynamic enterprises serving consumer needs. But, for "overriding social purposes" all too many are kept alive with dollar grants, credits, and government loans. Lockheed and Penn Central are only at the top of a long list of such waste of tax funds. Foundering financial institutions, such as the Franklin National Bank, are regularly rescued from the full consequences of their disastrous loan decisions by Federal Reserve bailouts and coverups.

Important establishment figures are calling for a revival of the Reconstruction Finance Corporation, the New Deal agency for "bailout capitalism". It would stand by to socialize the costs and risks of any firm deemed necessary to "the national interest", or any firm whose failure could result in a "hardship" for a significant sector of the economy. It does not take much imagination to figure out whose businesses will be "in the national interest" (a term fully as elastic as "for reasons of national security").

Instead of giving even a passing thought to the creation of the new RFC, it is vital that we recognize that decades of intervention into the market system have created deep economic misallocations—the very opposite of what happens in a purely free market system. And since there are now well-heeled vested interests benefiting from the assorted regulations, it becomes increasingly difficult to dismantle them. Remember the howl from the trucking and airline industries recently when it was suggested that deregulation begin in their protected sectors?

There must be an end to the privileges, inefficiencies, and exploitation which are the present results of the State's entanglement with the economy. To release the dynamic productive forces of the free market, there must be a complete separation of Economy and State. The businessman who does not use force or fraud should remain unhampered by government; as Robert Nozick (Harvard professor and Libertarian) put it, there should be no prohibition of "capitalist acts between consenting adults". Equally important, the government should not underwrite business in any manner: no favors, subsidies, bailouts, tariffs, regulatory agencies, credits to exporters, loan guarantees, and so on. As Libertarians dismantle these interventions with all deliberate speed, the day will be hastened when all businessmen operate solely in the competitive sector, and none remain in the privileged, protected sector.

Television and Radio

Have you ever complained about the lack of richness and diversity in your television programming? If you blamed the entrepreneurs who produce and distribute what you do see, you have blamed the wrong parties. The airwaves of this country have been nationalized for fifty years by the federal government, which took title to all radio and television channels and then granted licenses for the use of these channels to privately owned stations. Of course these licenses are a gigantic subsidy, as they are given out free, but they carry with them the federal government's assertion of power to regulate the stations minutely and continuously. Over the roof of every radio station hovers the threat of non-renewal of the license, which may well occur if the staion fails to have "balanced programming", provide a certain amount of "public service" announcements, grant "equal time" to every political candidate for the same office, censor "controversial" material, limit broadcasting at certain hours to material deemed suitable by the FCC for children, and so on.

Each of these rules promotes sameness and restricts diversity. For example, the "equal time" requirement all too frequently means the stations will not allow *any* political candidate to appear, because too much valuable broadcast time would be spent in accommodating *all* candidates. Hence a desirable public exposure of ideas and candidates is sacrificed.

The FCC has taken the view (at the instance of the networks) that the institution of pay television would cut the audience available to conventional broadcasting and hence weaken it. Therefore for a quarter of a century now the FCC has blocked the advent of pay TV. But what diversity would occur if that were available to us! Markets would be developed by producers of programs to limited but specific groups. There would be enough grand opera fans, for example, to justify the Metropolitan broadcasts in color on Saturday afternoons—many of us would gladly pay for the privilege of watching (there are enough auditors now for opera to have sustained the Texaco Saturday radio broadcasts for so long as to make it, I believe, the oldest continuing program in broadcast history). There would be sophisticated drama, coverage of lesser

known sporting events, telecasts of Broadway plays—
the list is of course endless. But no: the Federal Communications Commission will not permit pay TV.

It's an outrageous situation which most of us have tended to accept simply because it has so long been in existence. "But what would we think," asks Professor Murray Rothbard, "if all newspapers were licensed, the licenses to be renewable by a federal press commission, and with newspapers losing their licenses if they dare express an 'unfair' editorial opinion, or if they don't give full weight to public service announcements? Would this not be an intolerable, not to say unconstitutional, destruction of the right to a free press? Yet what we all consider intolerable and totalitarian for the press is taken for granted in the medium which is now the most popular vehicle for expression and education: radio and television."

Manifestly, the Federal Communications Commission and all of its unnecessary "powers" must be swept into history.

Agriculture

It's no news to you that you are paying more for the food you eat than you think justified. Part of the reason for this is the government's inflation of the money supply, discussed in the previous chapter. But another substantial reason is the government's agricultural policy which neatly has managed to make you as a consumer unhappy and the farmer as a producer unhappy.

As with most of its programs, the government's attitude toward agriculture is patchwork, and sometimes contradictory. There are quotas, for example, on the importation of sugar from abroad, so that the amount grown in this country is protected from price competition. When you go to the supermarket shelf, you are accordingly paying more for a bag of sugar than you would if this quota were abolished. The beet sugar farmers of this country are smiling. Are you?

Dairy farmers know of the endless list of new requirements in the construction and operation of milking facilities which are expensively pressed on them annually by the federal government and its meekly cooperative state agriculture departments. Tens of thousands have been driven out of business because they simply couldn't afford these innovations— boondoggles would be the word they would choose. On the other hand, for those who survive in the business the federal government has provided a "floor" for milk prices which prevents price competition in that area and hence raises the cost of milk for you and me in the supermarket. Indeed, it was the political manipulation of that minimum price which was a significant component of the Watergate scandal: remember the gigantic contributions to the Nixon campaign made by the milk producers, and even the bringing to trial of former Secretary of the Treasury John Connally on (not proved) charges that he connived in raising milk prices in trade for campaign support?

The pattern of regulation for a half-century and more by the U.S. Department of Agriculture has been to direct and limit production, and place a floor under prices. Extensive rules as to the amount of production and how it shall be obtained have been laid down which, though hated by most farmers, are accepted as the quid pro quo for an inept form of market price maintenance. The result has been the elimination of hundreds of thousands of farmers and creation of an artificial price level which has not satisfied farmers, yet costs consumers dearly.

The time has come to recognize that this wasteful intervention in the agricultural economy of the United States by the federal government has been, on net balance, counter-productive. It is time to formulate a policy which with all deliberate speed will disentangle the federal government from agriculture. The purpose must be to advance to a system which will permit farmers to conduct their business as they see fit, on the one hand unfettered by restrictions on production and sale, and on the other hand unsupported by subsidies or the limitation of competition.

Conclusion

In this chapter I have visited a number of areas in which the intervention of the federal government has negatively influenced the degree of satisfaction we get out of our lives. I could go on to look at urban housing, for example, after decades of zoning laws, rent control, and urban renewal, or malpractice insurance for doctors, an industry severely regulated for scores of years. But I think I have reviewed enough problems to have demonstrated that *the* major problem of our time is that very intervention. Those who would like to continue analyzing specific problems may profit from the books listed in the footnote.[1] The rest of us will move on, having observed sufficient of the activities of that wizard in Washington. We recognize him for the humbug he is, and look forward to bringing an early end to his reign.

1. Rothbard, Murray, FOR A NEW LIBERTY; Friedman, Milton, THERE'S NO SUCH THING AS A FREE LUNCH; Lambro, Donald, THE FEDERAL RATHOLE.

"I have always given it as my decided opinion that no nation had a right to intermeddle in the internal concerns of another; that everyone had a right to form and adopt whatever government they liked best to live under themselves; and that, if this country could . . . maintain a strict neutrality and thereby preserve peace, it was bound to do so by motives of policy, interest, and every other consideration."

—George Washington
August 25, 1796

4

Foreign Policy

President Woodrow Wilson in 1917 reversed the basis of United States foreign policy prevailing since the days of Washington and Jefferson. The results have been disastrous.

Those early Presidents recognized that evil and predatory governments were abroad in the world. But they held that *this* country should ignore them (while holding our defenses high) and adopt a policy of benevolent neutrality toward the people who lived in their countries. They knew free trade and travel could not only benefit Americans, but offered in fact the only opportunity eventually to bring down totalitarian systems elsewhere. With that policy as the cornerstone of U.S. foreign relations,[1] America prospered, persons

---

1. Of course, there were two aberrations, each fortunately short: the wars with Mexico and Spain.

and capital poured to our shores, and a flowering of individual life-styles occurred such as had never been seen in the history of this planet.

Then Wilson, the professor from Princeton, succumbed to his grand dream. It was the mission of America to *make* the world safe for democracy. He half-intentionally maneuvered events, and half-intentionally let them be maneuvered to fit his design. By 1917 he was ready to precipitate this country into a purely European war, just another of a series stretching back to the crowning of Charlemagne in A.D. 800. As always there was a side which appeared "good" and one which did not. It took Wilson more than a month to persuade Congress, over the valiant opposition of such grand traditionalists as Senator "Fighting Bob" LaFollette, to declare war upon Germany.

We libertarians propose to reverse that vote and return to a strict policy of neutrality in other countries' affairs, of non-intervention in other peoples' wars, of free trade and travel throughout the world. We have before us the evidence of the unalloyed success of that policy for the U.S. for five generations, and the equally unalloyed catastrophe its opposite has brought upon us for two. Consider:

After sixty years of crippling and brutally destructive wars, commenced with the wish to "make the world safe for democracy", to "end all wars," to advance the "free world," and to "spread freedom throughout the globe," what has the U.S. accomplished? What kind of world was wrought at the cost of close to half a million American lives, of over a million Americans wounded, of hundreds of billions in American economic resources, of producing a swollen government at home at the expense of the liberties and the property of the individual citizen? What has the U.S. government accomplished at the terrible price of engendering a vast military machine, of enforced military service for American youth, of crippling American productivity with taxes, inflation, and controls, of diverting so much American investment and scientific personnel from peaceful production to the machines of war? If we look about us, we see a world where dictatorship has never been stronger, where war has never been more threatening or fearful. After over a half-century of on-and-off war, we and the rest of the world have lost much of our freedom, rather than gained it. And universal peace is far away.

From the American Revolution to the end of the 19th century, the United States was only rarely involved in major foreign wars; until 1898 only the 1845 war with Mexico marred an otherwise enviable record of non-intervention. In 1898 both Democrats and Republicans clamored for military intervention in Cuba for 'humanitarian' reasons, and a Republican President, William McKinley, took the United States to war with Spain under the battle cry of "Remember the *Maine!*" Exactly who sank the *Maine* is still a mystery but we do know that the human cost of the Spanish-American War was 2,910 Americans killed.

In 1916 Democratic President Woodrow Wilson was reelected under the slogan 'He kept us out of war' - referring to the then raging war in Europe. Yet in 1916 during the campaign, Wilson was arming the United States for war and after reelection in April 1917 formally asked Congress to declare war in order, in Wilson's own words '. . . to bring peace and safety to all nations and make the world itself at last free . . .' The human cost of this European intervention was 50,585 Americans killed.

In 1940 Democratic President Franklin D. Roosevelt took two Republicans, Stimson and Knox, into his Cabinet and campaigned for reelection on the theme of non-intervention. 'Your boys are not going to be sent into any foreign wars', the American public was assured. By December 1941 Roosevelt with his bipartisan Cabinet had by intervention in the Sino-Japanese struggle maneuvered United States entry into a war with Japan and Germany. The human cost of the Roosevelt liberal interventionist policy was 292,100 Americans killed.

On June 14, 1949 conservative Republican John Foster Dulles left Washington D.C. for Korea. His mission? In Dulles' own words, he went to Korea to 'wage peace'. In Tokyo on June 21 Dulles predicted "positive action by the United States to preserve peace in the Far East", and a week later on June 27 the United States intervened militarily in the Korean War. The human cost of the Korean War? 40,181 Americans killed.

This bipartisan approach to foreign wars was repeated in the 1960s and the 1970s, under liberal Democrat President Lyndon Baines Johnson and conservative Republican President Richard Nixon. Unable to decide whether to win or lose the Vietnamese War, a bipartisan stop and go military policy cost 30,570 Americans killed under President Johnson and over 16,000 Americans killed under President Nixon. The Soviet Union supplied over 80 per cent of the supplies and weapons for North Vietnam, while the United States provided almost all the supplies and weapons for South Vietnam. Now coming to light is the support given to these presidents by American businessmen from Standard Oil, General Electric, Ford Motor Company and so on. Is it coincidental that they profited generously from the massive defense orders generated by the years of intervention in the name of peace, aptly called "perpetual war for perpetual peace"!

In brief, this century's much applauded bipartisan Democratic-Republican foreign policy has cost 432,246 Americans their lives in addition to millions of other Americans wounded and maimed for life.

A particularly distressing example of the bankruptcy of our contemporary foreign policy was the response of the President of the United States to the crumbling of that policy in Southeast Asia in the spring of 1975. The United States had intervened massively in Vietnam and in the rest of Indochina since World War II, and especially since the 1950s. Disregarding the sound advice of such men as Herbert Hoover and General Douglas MacArthur never to get involved in a land war in Asia, Presidents Kennedy, Johnson, and Nixon did.

With the American dead in Vietnam lie hundreds of

thousands of Vietnamese. Over a hundred billion dollars were extracted from American taxpayers to prop up a government which while doubtless preferable to communist North Vietnam, was still by American standards intolerably totalitarian. In the end all that effort had been wasted, poured down the proverbial rathole.

And *yet,* with the consequences of his and his predecessors' foreign policy crashing about him, what did President Ford do? He could only pathetically repeat, like a broken record, the same outworn catchwords, the same shibboleths that had brought him and the U.S. to this pass: a call for "one more chance" and for another $700 million from the American taxpayer (after the South Vietnamese army had left over a billion dollars of American arms and equipment behind in their flight): a call for propping up the South Vietnamese semi-totalitarian regime in order to "spread freedom throughout the world": a reiteration of the domino theory, such that if Saigon fell, Sacramento would be soon to follow: and an attack upon opponents of the war identified as "neo-isolationists" somehow being responsible for the mess that Mr. Ford's predecessors and the interventionists had brought upon all of us. The one thing that President Ford did *not* then do was to reevaluate the entire direction of American foreign policy.

But that is the one big thing that we *must* do. As in the case of our economic mess, America can *not* afford superficial reforms or half-way solutions. The entire thrust and purpose of American foreign policy must be changed. We must stop the interventionist policy of wasting American blood and treasure in an attempt to dictate to people and to nations all over the globe. We must return to the traditional foreign policy that America had pursued for over a century of peace and neutrality with all nations, of abstaining from governmental meddling in the affairs of other countries.

Our traditional foreign policy was that of live and let live, and it was a moral and non-aggressive policy that *worked,* that brought us over a century of peace, prosperity, and freedom, of harmonious economic trade and interchange with all nations, regardless of their social and political systems. The traditional American foreign policy was also a libertarian one: to allow peaceful freedom of trade between us and all other nations; but to abstain rigorously from any *political* intervention in their affairs. President Jefferson expressed this policy in his first inaugural address: "peace, commerce, and honest friendship with all nations; entangling alliances with none." And President Washington, in his Farewell Address, said, "The great rule of conduct for us, in regard to foreign nations is in extending our commercial relations to have with them as little *political* connection as possible . . . Why, by interweaving our destiny with that of any part of Europe, entangle our peace and prosperity in the toils of European ambition, rivalship, interest, humor or caprice?" Today, he would have added the words "Asian" and "African" after the word "European".

Because today, after America's experience in the twentieth century, the virtues of America's older noninterventionist foreign policy are clear. We can see that the indispensable corollary of rolling back government at home is rolling back government abroad. Getting the government out of our affairs at home is part and parcel of getting it out of the affairs of other peoples.

Libertarians say we have had enough. Both Democrats and Republicans have irresponsibly and deliberately injected the United States into wars and conflicts around the world without achieving either peace or stability. From time to time, the big party power structure produces a devil and uses it to whip up public antagonism. The Kaiser was the devil in 1917, Hitler and Tojo in 1941, the Communists in 1950 and 1965. Libertarians argue that we need no more foreign devils, and the time has come to return home and get the bureaucrats and politicians off our backs.

To fight these foreign wars, successive administrations have lied to the American people - always under the guise of 'national security' - about the causes of war and then proceeded to set the stage for the next war. The example as I write in early 1976 is the emplacement of 200 American technicians in the Suez Canal. These American technicians are hostages. The Israelis and the Arabs have well qualified technicians to man electronic consoles in the buffer zone. The U.S. technicians are a trip wire to ensure that the United States will be directly involved in the next Middle East war. The Kissinger agreement guarantees war, or continuing massive interventions to stave it off, because neither Israel nor the Arab states will act in American interests. They will quite understandably act in their *own* interests, and each will strive to bring the United States into a Middle East war on its side. Put yourself in the position of either the Arabs or the Israelis, with what *you* believe to be legitimate aspirations which can be attained with the military power of the United States on *your* side. Would you not be working today and tonight to involve the U.S.?

What does the Libertarian Party propose as an alternative?

The philosophical base of the broad based libertarian movement emphasizes individual action and individual freedom. We are skeptical of big government and our objective is to minimize the state. We particularly object to the use of the state mechanism, which is the cause of our foreign policy problems, not the cure. We want liberty and peace, not coercion and war.

Accordingly, in the field of foreign affairs we will replace intervention by strict non-intervention. The frontiers of the United States are geographically well defined; the only possible necessary government presence outside them is a diplomatic presence. Foreign relations conducted by the State will be replaced by foreign relations by individuals, groups and voluntary associations in an atmosphere of voluntary mutual exchange with their foreign counterparts.

We propose to attain this situation of no foreign affairs in an orderly and responsible manner. Instead of killing Americans and others in "perpetual peace" programs which always degenerate into war, we propose to achieve peace simply by abstaining from overseas intervention. No Americans are going to be sent abroad to get killed or involved in war.

Our program of action calls for the transformation of the Department of Defense from a mixed aggressive-defensive mode to "porcupine status"; that is, a defense force which will *only* respond to foreign aggression aimed at the geographical territory of the United States. The Defense Department in a Libertarian Administration will be just that, a *defense* department with no capability for offensive action, but with a decisive capability to deter foreign aggression, and to defeat it if in a remote event deterrence fails. We would be alert for genuine possibilities for removing the spectre of nuclear confrontation through disarmament agreements consistent with maintaining such a deterrence.

Our foreign policy will be revamped to give it a consistently libertarian thrust and purpose: The U.S. government will totally abstain from military intervention. It will quit meddling in the domestic politics of foreign countries and stop propping up foreign governments. The U.S. government will grant diplomatic recognition to all existing governments on the basis of *de facto* authority alone. That recognition will occur despite our distaste - even loathing - of the governments of such as Cuba or Rhodesia. We will let the example of a free society in the United States be our primary contribution to raising the quality of life in the world. It was Jefferson's hope that the United States would be a beacon light of liberty in the world and that the achievements of free individuals here would inspire others. It is to this noble vision of America's potential influence that we should return.

In addition, American foreign policy must include strict adherence to free trade principles. This means allowing trade with all countries (including South Africa on the one hand and the Soviet Union on the other). It also means that Americans may invest abroad - as and where they wish - but at their own risk, unprotected by the U.S. government.

Under a program of universal and if necessary unilateral free trade the U.S. government would impose no tariffs or quotas on imports. Exchange across international boundaries would be free and prices paid by American consumers for many goods, from cotton shirts to automobiles, would of course be lower as a result.

And what about U.S. participation in international organizations? The United Nations is a den of power politics operated at the expense of the taxpayers of the world. With its free swinging debates and verbal aggression it exasperates and exaggerates differences between countries until the differences threaten to erupt in conflict. The best interests of all require the quieting of this hotbed of discord. We propose therefore to withdraw from the United Nations and its auxiliary organizations. We will thus save the American taxpayer approximately one half billion dollars almost immediately. We will also withdraw from the International Monetary Fund, the World Bank and similar international organizations which in practice are engines of inflation and yield few if any practical benefits to society. International loans as far as this country is concerned will be undertaken only on the international private capital markets. Following the termination of the Federal Reserve Bank and a return to a gold standard, currencies will exchange in terms of a genuine market commodity.

Adherence to free trade also requires abolition of all export subsidies and loan guarantees. For example, this means abolition of the Export-Import Bank, whose government-backed loans divert private investment money from more productive uses.

Intelligence activities of the U.S. government will be limited to collection of signs of possible offensive action against the United States.

I do not of course underestimate world communism. The Soviet Union has the same aggressive proclivities and potential as other statist regimes. The United States has since the 1920's largely *built* the Soviet Union's technology with that developed in an enterprise society. If the Soviet Union stands on its own technical feet without our financial and technical subsidies, the inefficiencies of a socialist economy will effectively inhibit any overseas adventures it may contemplate.

"Collective security" has been a favorite slogan of the U.S. government officials who have handled foreign affairs since World War II. In essence, collective security is the policing of international conflicts by allied powers or by some agency they have created. Using collective security to impose some preferred order on the world is the goal of both the North Atlantic Treaty

Organization, which is dominated by the United States, and of the Warsaw Pact organization, which is dominated by the U.S.S.R. It was also the vision which inspired the Holy Roman Empire, the League of Nations, and the United Nations.

Yet too often the goal of *imposing* peace obscures the potential of collective security to produce a war; Henry Kissinger himself noted in his book *A World Restored,* "a system of collective security justified universal interference." The inherent tendency of collective security systems is to meddle in every matter which might threaten the existing international order. No conflict can be purely local. A minor incident easily becomes the spark of a world war. In addition to increasing the likelihood of world war, collective security arrangements also lessen the political liberties of Americans by setting up an automatic mechanism for involvement in war, without public debate and critical evaluation.

America's two best known alliance systems—NATO and SEATO—were designed as regional collective security groupings. At the time Truman set up NATO Senator Robert A. Taft, Sr., warned that it would give the executive branch *carte blanche* for decades to draw the U.S. into war without specific congressional consideration and that in fact it might create the risk of a Soviet reaction. SEATO was a copy set up by John Foster Dulles as a method for intervening in Southeast Asia without congressional scrutiny, according to unpublished tape recordings lodged at Princeton University. The existence of SEATO commitments made it easier for the U.S. government to get deeper and deeper into Indochina. The Vietnam mess was one of the bitter fruits of collective security.

The Truman Doctrine provided military aid to governments threatened with domestic insurrection; the Eisenhower Doctrine promised military intervention to support governments facing internal rebellion. Both Truman's interference in the Greek civil war and Eisenhower's landing of troops in Lebanon are precisely the sort of policing-of-the-world that should be abandoned.

A vitally important matter is rolling back the power, size, and influence of the biggest lobby for intervention and unchecked Executive power—the military-industrial complex.

The military-industrial complex includes the military itself.

Each year the Pentagon spends more than the annual income of every corporation in America. It spends funds upon twenty thousand business firms, which (with their employees) live off money taken from American taxpayers. The military-industrial complex is by no means a free-market phenomenon. Instead it resembles a royal court in which a king (the Pentagon) grants favors to his favorites (in the arms and military-support industries).

Libertarian views of these matters happily run counter to those held by many Congressmen in Washington. Despite some grumbling during the Indochina War, most Senators and Congressmen were delighted to let the President take full charge of foreign affairs. They rushed to support any President's actions before they knew the facts, just as they stampeded to support the Gulf of Tonkin resolution which justified President Johnson's escalation of the Vietnam War. Henry Kissinger, a long-time Rockefeller protege, has publicly attacked Congress for "meddling" in foreign policy and has expressed the view that the President should "rule" with a strong hand. Vice-President Rockefeller bitterly criticized Congress for causing the "loss" of Vietnam; for his own excellent reasons, Rockefeller would like to see power concentrated in the Executive.

Only an aroused and informed public can reverse the tide of Big Brother expansion via interventionist foreign policy. Unless we realize that the Barry Goldwaters and the Hubert Humphreys of American politics agreed all along on the need for a strong national-security state we will be unable to begin the search for alternatives beyond the old ideological labels of "conservative" and "liberal".

There are several practical steps which can be taken to begin this process. First, the Constitution should be read literally. Only Congress can declare war: Presidential "police actions" without Congressional authorization, such as the Korean and the Vietnamese Wars are more appropriate to despotic imperialist powers than to free societies. And of course Presidents should have absolutely no authority to carry on secret, CIA-funded wars.

In line with this diminution of executive authority the President should be forbidden from making secret commitments. The lessons of the secret treaties of

World War I may be old, but should not be forgotten, as the Kissinger Near Eastern diplomacy has served to remind us. Since World War I, Presidents have by-passed Congressional authority not only by using their supposed power as Commander-in-Chief, but also by making private agreements with other heads of state. For example, President Truman agreed, without the consent of Congress, to subsidize Spain in return for military bases. Such executive agreements undermine the Senate's power to publicly scrutinize and then reject or ratify treaties.

Something akin to the Constitutional amendment offered by Senator John Bricker (R-Ohio) which would have made all executive agreements subordinate to the Constitution, should be adopted.[2]

This step by step first stage program will begin to replace an aggressive interventionist stance with a peaceful non-interventionist stance. Libertarians believe that relationships among countries should evolve naturally and not as some artificial creature from the minds of academics, balance of power theoreticians, politicians and corporate socialists.

The libertarian alternative is clean and simple: we do not intervene in the affairs of other countries. The Middle East problem is to be solved by the people of the Middle East, not by anyone else. The affairs of Africa will be settled by Africans. The affairs of Latin

2. In February 1954, the Bricker Amendment fell only one vote short of the two-thirds necessary for approval by the Senate. I wrote a book analyzing this proposal in 1955: *Treaties Versus the Constitution,* Caxton Printers, Ltd.

America by Latin Americans. The affairs of Europe by Europeans. As a nation we must not intervene, although, as in the Middle East conflict, nothing should prevent private aid and assistance. Bluntly, the United States will stop poking its nose into every problem around the world.

Only a Libertarian Administration will halt our present conflict-generating interventionist stance. We will replace intervention by non-intervention. Militarism by voluntarism. State agreements by individual agreements. Coercive political action by voluntary mutual exchange. The power of the state will be diffused and foreign affairs will be reduced to the decentralized voluntary affairs of individuals in a free society.

We libertarians are wary of those who use the slogans of collective security to justify war and empire. Arnold Toynbee used to claim that the security of the British Empire was the supreme interest of the whole world. American politicians are no less inclined to identify with supreme goodness either American policy or the policy of alliances to which the U.S. belongs. Woodrow Wilson once said that the U.S. had bombarded the port of Veracruz, Mexico, in 1914 in order "to serve mankind." Rather than being seduced by the ever less credible calls of such men, we should heed Jefferson's warning against entangling alliances and strive for an internationalism built on peace, neutrality, cultural exchanges, and trade.

"Human liberty requires liberty of tastes and pursuits; of framing the plan of our life to suit our own character; of doing as we like, subject to such consequences as may follow: without impediment from our fellow creatures, so long as what we do does not harm them, even though they should think our conduct foolish, perverse, or wrong."

—John Stuart Mill
On Liberty

"To protect men from their own folly is to people the world with fools."

—Herbert Spencer

"Puritanism: the haunting fear that someone, somewhere, may be happy."

—H. L. Mencken

5

The Overreach of the Criminal Law

Our system of criminal law was designed to protect our persons and property. But offenses involving violent crimes - robbery, rape, aggravated assault and murder - have been occurring at a rapidly increasing rate over the last two decades.

The unhappy fact is that the criminal-justice system appears to be as effective as the U.S. Postal Service in doing the job it is designed to do. Only a small fraction of burglars, rapists and muggers are caught. Only twenty persons are even *arrested* for every hundred violent crimes committed. And naturally even less are convicted and fined or imprisoned. Gregory Krohm of Virginia Polytechnic Institute estimates that the chances an adult burglar will go to prison for any single job are 24 in 10,000. And for a juvenile offender under seventeen the risk of punishment is about half of that.

Astonishingly, at the same time that the criminal justice system is failing to serve its basic function, it is called upon to control matters of private morality. Since the justice system so used is diverted from its legitimate task of protecting the public this tendency is both costly and harmful. Diversion today may in fact be the main cause of the system's failure to protect the public.

It's time to rethink what is involved in the tendency to rely on the criminal law to control the private, consensual conduct of individuals—and what the consequences are of such use of the criminal law. We've lost sight of what was the common wisdom of our libertarian forebears in this regard. Recall John Stuart Mill's words in *On Liberty*:

> "The only purpose for which power can be rightfully exercised over any member of a civilized community, against his will, is to prevent harm to others. His own good, either physical or moral, is not a sufficient warrant. He cannot rightfully be compelled to do or forbear because it will be better for him to do so, because it will make him happier, because, in the opinions of others, to do so would be wise or even right. These are good reasons for remonstrating him, but not for compelling him or visiting him with any evil in case he do otherwise."

In viewing this matter it is important to recognize what criminal conduct is and how it is determined to be criminal. The short definition of crime is, simply, conduct that violates the criminal law. What the criminal

78

law *is* varies from place to place. In all modern societies, it includes such basic offenses as violence to the person (murder, assault) and wrongful deprivation of property (robbery, fraud).[1] But today there is the vast and continuing expansion of the criminal law to regulate voluntary transactions between individuals which involve no other persons than themselves. The Calvinists, as former Senator Eugene McCarthy remarked to me, are always with us.

I generally agree with Mill's criterion for limiting the criminal law to regulating conduct only "to prevent harm to others." It is the fundamental moral right of individuals to live their lives as they choose, so long as they do not forcibly interfere with others. The basic principle which should determine the sphere of the criminal law is that *no consensual adult conduct should be punishable as a crime.* The use of criminal legislation to protect people from themselves is a hallmark of an authoritarian approach to law. I flatly reject the idea of forcibly interfering with the lives of people who are not violating the equal rights of others.

What for all our sakes should be eliminated is that category of crimes now fashionably referred to as "victimless crimes" - because there is no victim in the sense of someone who will complain to the police. Typical

1. Of course many types of conduct which are commonly regarded as wrong are not ordinarily included in criminal statutes. For example, breach of contract is not a crime: "It is generally considered immoral to break a promise simply because it has become inconvenient to keep it (but) we do not put promise-breakers in jail." Packer, *The Limits of the Criminal Sanction.*

offenses generally considered "victimless crimes" include the supply of such goods or services as gambling, drunkenness, pornography, prostitution, homosexual acts, drugs, and other areas of private morality. But there are others, such as laws against usury to prohibit individuals from obtaining credit at a rate above that specified by law. This results in such consequences as a total unavailability of loans for mortgages to finance the purchase of a home in states that keep the maximum rate so low no lender is willing to lend out its funds. There are minimum wage laws regulating the level of wages which may be paid to a worker, frequently making it impossible for unskilled youths to secure employment, especially among blacks and other minority groups. Rent control laws artificially limit the rate of return to property owners and contribute to a deterioration of buildings and a scarcity of housing.

The usury laws which make criminals out of participants in voluntary economic transactions are justified on the paternalistic rationale that the state must act coercively to protect the welfare of each of us - that we cannot manage our affairs successfully otherwise. But all of that rests on flimsy assumptions and speculations actually derived from medieval attitudes rather than on sound economic data; the enormous weight of serious modern economic evidence is strongly to the contrary. Apart from any other consideration: isn't it prudent to view with caution the claim advanced by politicians that they know your best interest better than you - and that they will use force to make sure you conform?

I've heard it asserted that "victimless crimes" do involve victims, in the sense that an addict or a gambler is victimized by his vice. It's made even where the participants do not view themselves as victims. But the belief that someone who chooses to do something is victimized is a subjective determination based on the values of the observer. Why should not you and I, it is argued, who hate the very thought of drug addiction, and who would use every resource at our command to prevent a loved one's becoming addicted, why *shouldn't* we force our values on another? Hard case, I agree. But the rational answer is clear: force is no answer, love and persuasion may be.

Beyond the mere logical rightness of the individualistic libertarian position there are many ways in which the overreach of the criminal law aggravates the problem of crime. It is a fact, and not in the least paradoxical, that the use of the criminal law to control "victimless crimes" has produced an effect that is opposite to the intended one of reducing violent crime.

The costs of overloading the criminal justice systems have become apparent. Here are some:

Criminal prohibition of goods or services such as drugs and gambling drives up their prices, by increasing the risk of engaging in these activities. Remember alcohol Prohibition?

Those who meet the public demand for the prohibited goods or services are, by definition, criminal. Profitable criminal activity leads to the development and expansion of large-scale organized criminal groups.

People engaging in consensual conduct which is criminalized tend to associate with others who are involved in really serious criminal activities, which engenders a widespread disrespect for the criminal law in general, and therefore a resultant increase in the commission of serious crimes.

And naturally police resources are limited. Their efforts to deal with serious crimes are diverted by attempts to enforce laws against private consensual conduct, which leads to a lower rate of apprehension of serious crimes. The high number of cases involving "victimless crimes" imposes enormous pressure on the courts, which causes a backlog in both civil and serious criminal cases.

Because there is no complainant to report the crime and assist in prosecuting the offender, and because there is widespread acceptance of other peoples' right to indulge in such activities as gambling, prostitution, and marijuana smoking, laws against private consensual conduct are extremely difficult to enforce. That in turn leads to police reliance on informers and eavesdropping, and the use of illegal searches and perjury. It also produces, for economic motives and for the honest reason that many of the police don't think these activities seriously wrong, large-scale bribery of the police.

These are some of the costs, and you and I are forced to pay the high costs of their enforcement. You and I are subjected to a higher risk of serious criminal acts. And you and I find the courts to be less responsive to our needs because of the backlog of criminal cases. And look at the proliferation of lawyers in this country during the last generation! They are there because of the proliferation of laws.

Let's examine the wisdom of forbidding by law a few types of conduct.

The hypocrisy of anti-gambling laws should be obvious to everyone. A great many states make perfectly legal a few forms of gambling with a high return to the government—and forbid anyone else to engage in gambling games or bet upon sports. New York State comes immediately to mind as the ultimate in this case: the state-owned Off-Track Betting Corporation throws open its windows early in the morning, but beware any honest citizen who attempts to go into competition by making private book! Betting on horse races is legal, with a fat percentage going to the state, but not betting on dog races or human sports. The so-called numbers game is vigorously prosecuted, but a state-owned lottery which doesn't pay winners much differently sells its tickets in practically every newsstand in the state. Need I say that there is no moral justification for these discriminatory laws? Need I say that legalized gambling would produce pressure for honest games, because there would be legal recourse in case of crookedness, and because competition would require honesty? Need I say that another prop to serious criminal activity would be removed? A Libertarian President would seek repeal of any and all acts of Congress restricting the flow of gambling devices between the states, or restricting the flow of information for wagers between the states. I hope this would be a reform that would lead to widespread repeal of anti-gambling statutes amongst the states.

It's a cliche that prostitution is the world's oldest profession. Whether we like it or not it's here to stay, as are fornication, homosexuality, and other sexual conduct which, even though indulged in between consenting adults, is regarded as immoral by a large segment of Americans. Should the law forbid them? Supposing homosexuals happened to be the majority in your community and passed an ordinance forbidding heterosexual marital sexual activity. We would snort with derision at the ludicrousness of such an idea. But why? Wouldn't that be a case of a majority imposing its moral standards on an unwilling minority? And isn't that exactly what is being done throughout America now with anti-gay laws and anti-prostitution laws? Wouldn't it be wise, and the most peace-making solution, to leave moral standards to be determined by the individuals involved? Certainly removing the government from this area would remove an element of confusion about moral standards, to let the issues be faced squarely on their merits. Further, of course, there is the dividend that law enforcement procedure personnel would be free to spend more time deterring violent sexual crimes, such as rape, rather than pursuing individuals who quite literally are doing no harm to anyone.

Manifestly "anti-smut" laws are an attempt to impose the moral views of some upon all. I believe they fall in the same classification as the happily dead "Jim Crow laws", which imposed the racial views of some whites upon all whites and blacks. Who is to define pornography? The Supreme Court has wrestled with this question for a couple of decades and gotten nowere. The plain fact is that the determination of what is pornographic is wholly subjective, and therefore wholly a matter of political whim. In Denmark the Parliament a few years ago was sensible enough to throw the whole business overboard: it repealed all laws restricting the sexual content of reading material. The result at first was a flood of pornographic publications: most everyone was eager to see erotic, titillating material. But within a year production and consumption of pornographic material in Denmark fell to a point substantially below where it had been prior to its legalization. It appears that if you've seen one dirty book you've seen them all. The lure of the illegal no longer existed. The same would happen in America, and therefore libertarians would propose the repeal of all attempts to restrict the content of reading material.

What is the greatest single cause of violent crime—now at the highest level in the United States in its history? It is the need of drug addicts to raise funds to support their habits. The President's Council on Drug Abuse reported that as of 1975 about $6.3 billion in property damage or loss in that year alone was caused by addicts seeking the price of their illicit nirvana. In addition, you and I paid out about $630 million in court costs related to the futile attempt to stop the traffic in, and punish the traffickers of, hard drugs—

for a grand total of approximately $7 billion a year.

Now, the addict curled in his corner enjoying his foolish stupor is no danger to you or me whatsoever. He presents a very real danger when he goes after us with a knife or a club or a gun to obtain the money needed to support his habit for the day. I'm told that figure may run close to $150 currently. $150! For a tiny amount of a substance which can today be obtained in a British drugstore for about 50 cents! What's the reason for the difference?

As is obvious, the reason is the *illegality* of heroin. Heroin was perfectly legal in this country from its beginning until 1914, when the Harrison Narcotics Act was passed. In that year there were just 2,000 drug addicts in America. But just as with alcohol prohibition, driving consumption underground had the effect of dramatically increasing both cost and abuse. Organized crime appeared for the first time in this country during the 1920s to supply a demand for alcohol, and of course it is still with us. With the repeal of the alcohol prohibition laws in 1933, organized crime turned its attention to the enormous sums of money available for supplying illegal heroin. The price was high and was driven higher. Some addicts were and are required by suppliers to "push" the drug upon non-users in order to obtain their fix—thereby creating new markets with awesome financial potential. Most addicts are eventually virtually forced to commit criminal acts in order to obtain the price of a fix. The profit is so high that organized crime has managed to increase the number of addicts in this country to upwards of 300,000 today!

Contrast the English experience. In 1914 the Parliament of that country contemplated a similar drug prohibition law, but accurately foresaw the consequences we have reaped in this country. It instead passed a very mild statute requiring that any addict go to a doctor and obtain a prescription for his daily fix of heroin, which could thereafter be filled at the corner drugstore. The profit potential in the creation of new drug users never came into being, and the official count of the number of addicts in Britain in the early 1970s was about 300, up from 200 in 1914!

Isn't the lesson obvious? That it is government intervention in the field of drugs which has created this monstrous problem? And that it is only by decriminalizing heroin (in the sense of repealing drug prohibition laws, rather than merely lessening penalties) that we will at once stop the creation of new addicts, end overnight a gigantic amount of crime, and at last open the door to allow those whose lives are currently ruined by the new Prohibition to reenter the productive life of this country.

Of course there must be adequate laws to protect all of us from damage by persons under the influence of any drug, alcohol, pot, or heroin. For example, there must be stringent laws dealing with operating motor vehicles while so influenced.

*   *   *

And so it will go with respect to every area in which

the government has entangled itself in the daily lives of the citizens of this country to their enormous detriment.

Because I believe in the right of individuals to control their own lives, I advocate a massive overhaul of the criminal law. Since the beginning of these United States the government has been forbidden to regulate private conduct in matters of religion. That is an apt model to guide us. Why should government have any greater power to exert control over purely private conduct in nonreligious areas?

I hardly need say that the case for removing the government from these areas does not add up to my advocacy of any particular conduct. But the fact that I do not approve of your visiting a prostitute or gigolo, using LSD, or borrowing money at 18% annual interest, is not the point. The point is whether we really want Big Brother to decide for us. As individuals, you and I may and do strongly disapprove of foolish conduct. But we have no right to force our neighbors to pay high taxes to attempt to gratify our views by interfering with the private conduct of others.

I say again: in these matters there *are* serious issues of moral conduct. Fortunately there are many institutions other than government that can appropriately deal with these matters. To handle the task of teaching and maintaining desirable standards of behavior, logic and experience dictates reliance on the individual, the home, the family, the schools, the churches and synagogues, and the almost infinite number of other voluntary associations which now exist in every nook of this country.

People must again be allowed to live their lives free of the coercion of the criminal law unless they invade the rights of others. The difficulty lies in removing the mantle of myth, prejudice and politics from the issue of "crime control". I think we will succeed.

"We now have that systematic theory (of liberty); we come, fully armed with our knowledge, prepared to bring our message and to capture the imagination of all groups and strands in the population. All other theories and systems have clearly failed: socialism is in retreat everywhere and notably in Eastern Europe; liberalism has bogged down in a host of insoluble problems; conservatism has nothing to offer but sterile defense of the status quo. Liberty has never been fully tried in the modern world; libertarians now propose to fulfill the American dream of liberty and prosperity for all."

— Murray N. Rothbard in
For a New Liberty

6

A New Dawn

Says the Old Testament:

The elders of Israel came to Samuel and said unto him "Now make us a king to judge us like all the other nations."

And Samuel answered with the words of the Lord, saying, "This will be the manner of the king that would reign over you:

He will take your sons and make them his charioteers. He will set them to reap his harvest and make his instruments of war. He will take your daughters to be cooks.

And he will take your fields and your vineyards and give them to his supporters. He will take a tenth of your produce and give it to his staff. He will take the tenth of your sheep: and you shall be his servants.

And you shall cry out in that day because of your king which you shall have chosen."[1]

This Biblical description of government's nature is the earliest I know of, and it raises a question still with us. Why is government not recognized as a violent and demanding interloper in human affairs? Why would anyone willingly submit to its false Authority?

The Israelites had lived and prospered for centuries without a State, but when they asked Samuel for a king, he really laid it on the line: your king will take your lands, your children, your goods and your freedom, and you shall cry out in that day.

For "king" we moderns substitute President and Congress, Supreme Soviet, City Manager, State Governor, County Supervisors, Zoning Boards, or any other "authority". But today as historically, the State remains an instrument of coercion, war, privilege and economic exploitation. Yet so many people have not seen it so. Nay, they say, we will have a king over us.

That calls for an explanation. As we have in this short book alone demonstrated, few government activities can be justified in terms of results. To conclude that it delivers the goods, on time and as promised, requires a pathological aversion to reality. It is actually a matter of everyday and notorious fact that politicians are a gamey breed whose promises are worthless and whose only competence is in compelling, prohibiting, frequently stealing, selling favors, and occasionally

1. Adapted from the King James version, I Samuel 4-20.

kissing babies; that passing laws and creating bureaus cannot add one jot to human happiness; that governments habitually engage in aggression, grand larceny, cheating, lying, counterfeiting, bullying, meddling and other pursuits immediately recognized, in the private sphere, as nasty and immoral. Why don't people compare political promises with government results?

Part of the reason obviously is that some people don't see government as it is because they don't *want* to. They believe the State is what they want it to be—a godlike Authority, a last resort in all human difficulties. While there is no rational reason for believing that a policeman is our best defender or that a judge offers true justice simply by virtue of living at taxpayer expense, some Americans are so unaware of their personal strength they have been brought to accept propaganda to the contrary.

Another part of the reason is that from ancient times all governments have been at pains to theologize themselves and disguise their nature with the kind of rituals still enacted daily. The task of persuading you that they do in fact rule you has engaged the ingenuity of politicians for thousands of years, and by now they have spun a fine web of majesty and mystery and magnificence to hide the facts. During the last hundred years Washington has cloaked itself in a dazzling array of rituals, doctrines, protocols, monuments, flags, titles and other such fustian to reinforce popular belief in its omnipotent character.

What used to be tribute collected at spearpoint has

become, with centuries of refinement, "fiscal policy." A "planned economy" means politicians do the planning. "Public property" means property in the hands of politicians. "Monetary policy" means Federal Reserve Bank counterfeiting of actual commodity money. A "strongly expansionary monetary policy" means a lot of counterfeiting. A "welfare state" means more welfare for the State. A "statesman" is a politician so smooth he can get away with it. "Foreign powers" are rival gangs with whom "we" are either at war or in a state of negotiated peace, with the territories of each carefully—or for a purpose not-so-carefully—defined. "Taxation" is theft. Translating governmentese is very educational, and it's not hard once you get the hang of it. But it is all part of the act.

Such vaudeville would not turn many heads without the modern invention of the idea that "we" constitute the government and that the government is responsive to "our" needs and exists with "our" consent. Those notions are inherently ridiculous. You can tell perfectly well whether you are or are not a part of the government. If you have the power to tax, arrest, judge, command, or live off your neighbor, you are. If you are on the receiving end, you're not.

And from the time of the Declaration of Independence until as late as around 1920, most Americans *knew* that those notions were ridiculous. As a rule they then believed in their own self-authority, met their responsibilities, and maintained a healthy distrust of government. I'm certain it was chiefly this general distrust, combined with "the chains of the Constitu-

94

tion," (as Jefferson said) that kept the government's ambitions in check for a century and a half. Since both were swept away by the Wilson and Hoover administrations and their successors, governments at all levels have reached for, and got, unbelievable powers. It is as if this country, converted to belief in State Authority, is rapidly lapsing into senility. Without ever a meaningful political alternative in all those years the dreamland of conventional politics has come to be taken seriously.

Politicians have never stopped reminding you that you have the "right to vote," the right to choose your rulers. During those years they claimed that you were sovereign, that your view was "represented." By this dodge, the question of rule itself was safely confused and submerged under the question of *who* shall rule. Your supposed "right to vote" offered a very limited option to choose your rulers, and even the option to try to become a ruler; but it never offered you the choice of *not being* ruled.

But now at long, long last, as Americans find themselves on the Washington-provided slide to ruin, that alternative *has* appeared. Now there *is* a group of people who cherish their liberty and your liberty. Now all the hard lessons of history taught us from Samuel to Kissinger are embodied in a consistent outlook on America's problems.

There *is* a Libertarian political party. It seeks your vote, and more. It will grow as it has grown since 1971: from nothing to a fifty-state organization in four years. It will run some hundreds of persons for office devoted to its principles this year, and some thousands in election years to come.

The last major political party to arise in America is now disintegrating before our very eyes. When the Whig Party, the opposition to the Democratic Party, fell apart in the early 1850s, the Republicans appeared from nowhere. They lost their first try for the Presidency, and won the second to become the other major national party until now.

It takes no seer to realize that in the mid-1970s the Republican Party is in *its* death throes. Only a third of the national legislators are affiliated with it, and a handful of governors. The party stands for nothing and is finished.

And now the dynamic new Libertarian Party is arising with the likelihood of accomplishing what the Republicans did in their natal decade. Its success will be the product of the utter bankruptcy of Democratic and Republican politics. Their compulsive reliance upon force as the best solution to each new problem would, if unchecked, drag us all under as surely as quicksand. It is critical that the Libertarian Party succeed, for it alone lies between us and the dismal choice—down the years a bit, but not far—between total collectivism and violent upheaval.

It is not fanciful to say that the Libertarian Party offers one of the very few non violent opportunities for genuine choice in modern times. Most revolutions occur when governments have wrecked so many lives that guns succeed when backed by power-seekers with false yet seductive promises to provide "new" answers.

Let that never happen in this country! You and I, acting *together* can bring about a new dawn for America.

"I devour it...
It is, in a word,
indispensable."

Roger MacBride

Roger's talking about *Libertarian Review*—the premier commentary and review of books, ideas and the arts, written by and for libertarians.

Now, you can join Roger MacBride and be counted in the vanguard of the most exciting intellectual political movement of the century. For readers of *A New Dawn For America*, we've created a very special introductory offer: 12 issues of *Libertarian Review* for only $5. Since our regular annual subscription rate is $8, that means you get a *37% savings.*

Libertarian Review has been called the outstanding intellectual publication of the libertarian movement. Contributors include Murray N. *Rothbard*, Henry *Hazlitt*, Thomas *Szasz*, John *Hospers*, Nathaniel *Branden*, Robert *LeFevre*, Robert *Ekirch*, and many other distinguished writers.

Learn why Roger MacBride, the Libertarian Party's 1976 presidential candidate, says: *"Libertarian Review* is an indispensable door to [the intellectual aspect of the libertarian movement]. I devour it each month. Of course, I can't buy and read all of the books and records discussed, but from the *Review* . . . I'm abreast of current affairs and thought trends. To me it is, in a word, indispensable."

To take advantage of this special offer, tear out and mail this page today! Unconditional money-back guarantee if you're not completely delighted!

Libertarian Review

321

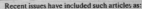
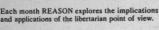

I want to be part of the battle of ideas for liberty. Enclosed is my *tax deductible* investment in freedom in the following amount:

☐ $2500 ☐ $1000 ☐ $500 ☐ $100 ☐ $50 ☐ Other $ _____

NOTE: Your contribution is *tax deductible* if check is made payable to the *Foundation for New Educational Projects, Inc.* Simply note on your check: "For the Center for Libertarian Studies."

☐ Please send me more information on the Center for Libertarian Studies.

Name _____

Address _____

City _____ State _____ Zip _____

Contributors of $100 or more become "Friends of the Center" and receive the CLS newsletter, the Journal of Libertarian Studies, all of the Center's Occasional Papers, invitations to seminars, discounts on Center publications, courses and lectures and a handsome card identifying them as a "Friend of Liberty."

The Center for Libertarian Studies has been organized to provide a permanent center for scholarly communication among libertarians. The Center will sponsor both the Libertarian Scholars Conferences and **The Journal of Libertarian Studies.** It is dedicated to facilitating other forms of libertarian scholarship and communication as well.

In order to best serve these ends, the Center for Libertarian Studies has been organized as a non-profit corporation. It has received the assistance of the Foundation for New Educational Projects, Inc. Checks made out to the Foundation for New Educational Projects, Inc., and earmarked for the Center for Libertarian Studies, are tax deductible.

To ensure the successful launching of its support for scholarly research into the discipline of liberty, the Center needs financial assistance. All contributions to the Center's cause, no matter how large or small, will be deeply appreciated by lovers and defenders of liberty everywhere.

Center for Libertarian Studies
200 West 58th Street   Suite 5D   New York, N.Y. 10019

A Free Book
with every four books you order!

1. **How to Start Your Own School**, Robert Love. Everything a parent or principal needs to know, by someone who did it himself. "An important and readable book that tells you how to do it.—*Human Events.* **$1.95**

2. **The Regulated Consumer**, Mary B. Peterson. The *Wall Street Journal* contributor shows how seven Federal regulatory agencies have been captured by the businesses they were supposed to regulate! How this hurts consumers everywhere, and what can be done about it. "This thoughtful, challenging book can perform a great service"— *Fortune.* **$2.95**

3. **The Gun Owner's Political Action Manual**, Alan Gottlieb. Everything a gun owner needs to know to be politically effective in the firearms freedom fight. Includes voting records of all Congressmen on every pro-/anti-gun vote, how to use the media, and a large reference section on publications and organizations. (July). **$1.95**

4. **The Hundred Million Dollar Payoff: How Big Labor Buys Its Democrats**, Douglas Caddy. "Explosive, extensively documented . . . likely to send shivers up some spines."—*Business Week.* **$2.95**

5. **The Libertarian Challenge: A New Dawn for America**, Roger MacBride. The Libertarian Party presidential candidate calls for a return to first principles. **$ .95**

6. **The Municipal Doomsday Machine**, Ralph de Toledano. Shows how close America is to a British-style Labor Government. **$1.95**

7. **Reflections on Economic Advising**, Paul W. McCracken. The former Chairman of the President's Council of Economic Advisers shows how our economy is managed. **$ .95** *(Booklet)*

8. **The Politicization of Economic Decisions**, Alan Walters, introduction by Harry Johnson. The economies of the West are being ruined by the substitution of politics for economics; the author shows how, and why. **$ .95** *(Booklet)*

VOTE FOR ONE.

☐ **Tweedledee (Republican)**
☐ **Tweedledum (Democrat)**
☐ **Roger MacBride (Libertarian)**

This November the American public will be offered—at last—
a real alternative to the traditional "lesser of two evils" when
they cast their votes for President. If you agree that we need a
new dawn in American politics, that it is time we regained
control over our own lives, then support Roger MacBride. Fill
out the coupon below and mail it today. You owe it to yourself.

> *"MacBride's views are like fresh air—almost like straight
> oxygen—and he has been winning converts from
> liberal and conservative camps at a surprising rate."*
> —National Observer

Enclosed is my contribution to the **MacBride/Bergland** campaign:

☐ $10   ☐ $25   ☐ $100   ☐ $250   ☐ $1000   ☐ $ _____

Name _____

Address _____

City _____ State _____ Zip _____

Occupation* _____

Business Address* _____

*Required by law for contributions over $100

Make checks payable to: **MacBride for President Committee**
1516 P Street, NW • Washington, D. C. 20005

Paid for by MacBride for President Committee, Robert H. Meier, Chairman

A copy of our report is on file with the Federal Election Commission and is available for
purchase from the Federal Election Commission, Washington, D. C.

VOTE FOR ONE.

☐ **Tweedledee (Republican)**

☐ **Tweedledum (Democrat)**

☐ **Roger MacBride (Libertarian)**

This November the American public will be offered—at last—a real alternative to the traditional "lesser of two evils" when they cast their votes for President. If you agree that we need a new dawn in American politics, that it is time we regained control over our own lives, then support Roger MacBride. Fill out the coupon below and mail it today. You owe it to yourself.

> "MacBride's views are like fresh air—almost like straight oxygen—and he has been winning converts from liberal and conservative camps at a surprising rate."
>
> —National Observer

Enclosed is my contribution to the **MacBride/Bergland** campaign:

☐ $10   ☐ $25   ☐ $100   ☐ $250   ☐ $1000   ☐ $ _____

Name _____

Address _____

City _____ State _____ Zip _____

Occupation* _____

Business Address* _____

*Required by law for contributions over $100

Make checks payable to: **MacBride for President Committee**
1516 P Street, NW • Washington, D. C. 20005

Paid for by MacBride for President Committee, Robert H. Meier, Chairman

A copy of our report is on file with the Federal Election Commission and is available for purchase from the Federal Election Commission, Washington, D. C.

"It is in the area of detail, in the fine tuning they have given their ideology in so few years, that the Libertarians' commitment to an undiluted human freedom is singulary impressive."

The Washington Post, January 25, 1976

LIBERTARIAN PARTY
National Membership Application

Name (Mr./Ms.) _____

Address _____

City _____ State _____ Zip _____

Occupation (optional) _____

Note: Membership includes a subscription to the LP NEWS. Make check payable to: Libertarian Party.

Type of Membership

☐ Student ($6)   ☐ Patron ($50)
☐ Regular ($8)   ☐ Lifetime ($200)
☐ Sustaining ($12) ☐ Life Sustaining ($1000)

Mail to:
Libertarian Party
1516 P St., N.W.
Washington, D.C., 20005

"I hereby certify that I do not believe in or advocate the initiation of force as a means of achieving political or social goals."

_____
(Signature)

Laissez Faire BOOKS

FOR A NEW LIBERTY   Murray Rothbard   8.95
Comprehensive exposition of the libertarian philosophy by a leading libertarian theoretician and economist. Includes discussion of the philosophy of natural rights as a basis for libertarianism and suggests private alternatives to government in such areas as roads, schools, courts, welfare, defense foreign policy and ecology.

LIBERTARIANISM   John Hospers   2.95
Comprehensive presentation of the libertarian political and economic philosophy by the Libertarian Party candidate for President in 1972.

THE MACHINERY OF FREEDOM   David Friedman   2.25
"The purpose of this book" says Friedman, "is to argue that a libertarian society would be both free and attractive, that the institutions of private property are the machinery of freedom, making it possible in a complicated and interdependent world, for each person to pursue his life as he sees fit."

ANARCHY, STATE AND UTOPIA   Robert Nozick   12.95
A carefully reasoned but somewhat technical examination of the nature of the State and of the concepts of individual rights and justice. A devastating libertarian challenge to the political and social positions of liberalism, socialism and conservatism. Winner of the National Book Award in Philosophy for 1974.

NO TREASON   Lysander Spooner   1.00
Classic and powerful polemic challenging the moral validity of the Constitution and arguing that the U.S. Government does *not* have the consent of the governed so is therefore no better than a gang of robbers and murderers.

EGALITARIANISM AS A REVOLT AGAINST NATURE   Murray Rothbard   2.50
15 essays examining such topics as the nature of the State, war, foreign policy, justice and egalitarianism.

THE INCREDIBLE BREAD MACHINE   Campus Studies Institute   1.95
Refutes many myths about laissez faire capitalism, dealing with issues such as monopolies, anti-trust laws, the Great Depression, minimum wage laws and inflation. Discusses the concepts of individualism and private property.

ECONOMICS IN ONE LESSON   Henry Hazlitt   1.50
The single best introduction to free market principles. Refutes many common myths about the desirability of government regulation of the economy in clear, easy to understand terms. Examines such issues as minimum wage laws, tariffs, and price controls.

THE ROAD TO SERFDOM   F.A. Hayek   3.25
A Nobel Prize-winning economist looks into the nature of socialism and fascism and demonstrates that planned economies inevitably lead to totalitarianism.

WHAT HAS GOVERNMENT DONE TO OUR MONEY?   Murray Rothbard   2.00
Examination of the nature and function of money and the destructive effects of government intervention into the monetary system.

WHAT YOU SHOULD KNOW ABOUT INFLATION   Henry Hazlitt   2.25
Succinct but thorough and clearly written presentation of the theory and practice of government money inflation.

THE ANTICAPITALIST MENTALITY   Ludwig von Mises   2.50
Analysis of psychological hostility to capitalism.

PLANNING FOR FREEDOM   Ludwig von Mises   3.00
13 essays covering a wide range of arguments defending the free market.

Please circle the titles you want to order and send this entire page to   SUB
LAISSEZ FAIRE BOOKS, Dept. M, 206 Mercer St., New York, N.Y. 10012.   TOTAL ....
POSTAGE— Add 50¢ for postage and handling on all orders ....   50¢

Name ....   TOTAL ....

Street ....   □ SEND FREE CATALOG

City/State .... Zip ....

This book can start a revolution*

A New Dawn for America:

The Libertarian Challenge

*and you can be a part of it. Distribute copies of *A New Dawn for America*—to your friends, associates, local media, social and political organizations. Let others know about the idea whose time is now—*Libertarianism!*

The generous discount schedule below also makes it possible for you or your club to *spread the Libertarian idea at a profit*. Order your copies now.

QUANTITY PRICES

1 copy $ .95	10 copies $ 7.50	100 copies $ 50.00
3 copies $2.50	25 copies $17.50	500 copies $200.00
5 copies $4.00	50 copies $30.00	1000 copies $350.00